MW01282942

SOLVING THE IMMIGRANT CHURCH CRISIS:

THE BIBLICAL SOLUTION

OF

PARALLEL MINISTRY (ACTS 6:1-7)

Ronald M. Rothenberg, Ph.D.

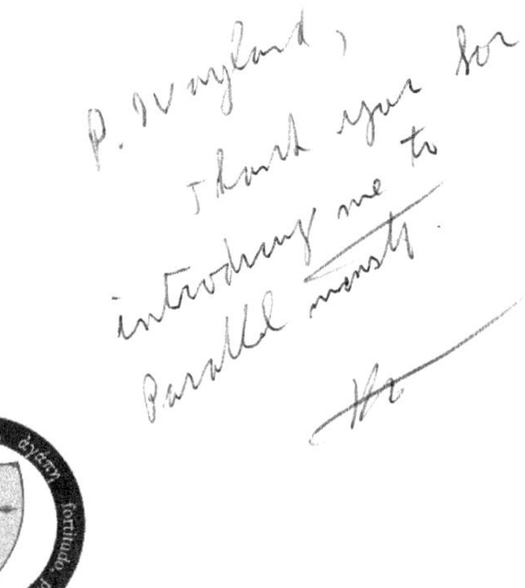

rmrothenberg@outlook.com
http://www.ronaldmrothenberg.com

Unless otherwise noted, all translations of Scripture are by the author from the 28th edition of the Nestle-Aland Greek New Testament.

ISBN-13: 978-1542787598
ISBN-10: 1542787599

Cover design and illustrations by Angela Lowe.

Printed by CreateSpace, Charleston SC, an Amazon.com Company.

To Joanna,

beloved wife, daughter of immigrants,

and

precious gift from God.

CONTENTS

LIST OF ILLUSTRATIONS

LIST OF TABLES

PREFACE

This book is the result of a decade of ministerial service to and over twenty years of experience with immigrant churches and parachurch ministries in the United States and around the world. It is also the culmination of experiences from having lived with my 1.5 generation Chinese wife and immigrant in-laws for sixteen years. This book is written for the pastors and educated laypeople of the immigrant church.

Hopefully, biblical guidance in this book may be found by those immigrant churches that know they are struggling to meet the needs of their children and sincerely do not know what they are supposed to do. Rather than looking around at what all the other immigrant churches are doing and repeating the failed mistakes of the past, perhaps they will follow the biblical model presented here. Instead of falling prey to biblically inconsistent sociological studies and theories that merely allow immigrants and their children to do what is culturally comfortable, this book challenges both groups to strive toward the biblical example of parallel ministry.

It is my wish that hope and direction from this commentary on the Bible can be found by frustrated immigrant pastors dealing with the seemingly enigmatic and rebellious children of their congregations, misunderstood local born minsters (English pastors) striving to meet the needs of immigrant children, discouraged immigrant children who feel unheard and their needs neglected, and immigrant parents heartbroken over the exodus of their children from the church and their loss of faith. May the Lord give you all the wisdom to discern the difference between the traditions of men or human culture and the traditions of Christ or the culture of the Kingdom (Mark 7:8; Col. 2:8). I also pray that you will have the faith, courage, and love to make the sacrifices necessary to obey God's model for the immigrant church in Acts 6:1-7.

I would like to thank a number of people for making this project possible. Wayland Wong first introduced me to the crisis of the immigrant church and taught me about parallel ministry. Curtis Lowe has faithfully mentored me during my entire Christian life and provided valuable feedback on the manuscript for this book. I would also like to thank the several immigrant pastors with whom I served, particularly Albert Lam, who patiently endured my early attempts to articulate the message of this book, and Isaac Hsu, who endured the implementation of a nearly complete parallel ministry at his church. The English pastors of the Evangelical Formosan Church (Tom Cheng, Bob Marshall, Eddie Sun, Roy Tinklenberg, and James Yu) shared their struggles with and views of how an immigrant church ministry should be structured. Additionally, Samuel Clintock (Romanian), Pierre St. Louis (Hattian), Davis Matthews (Indian), and the writings of Manuel Ortiz (Hispanic) helped me to understand that the crisis of the immigrant church is common to all ethnic groups. I am also grateful to the many immigrants and their children whom I served in pastoral ministry and who candidly shared their frustrations, heartaches, and dreams regarding the crisis of the immigrant church. My in-laws helped me to understand the immigrant perspective better. I would also like to thank Angela Lowe creating the cover and inside illustrations. This book would not be possible without my wife, Joanna, who has helped and supported me through many ministry endeavors, including long hours of editing various writing projects. Most of all, thanks to our Lord Jesus Christ for the experiences that contributed to this book and the opportunity to share it with His church.

Ronald M. Rothenberg
Grand Prairie, TX
2016

ABBREVIATIONS

ATAJ	*Asia Theological Association Journal*
BAPS	*The Book of Acts in Its Palestinian Setting*
BDAG	*A Greek-English Lexicon of the New Testament and Other Early Christian Literature*, 3rd ed.
BECNT	Baker Exegetical Commentary on the New Testament
BKC	*The Bible Knowledge Commentary*
BNTC	Black's New Testament Commentary
DSE	*Dictionary of Scripture and Ethics*
DTT	*Dictionary of Theological Terms*
EBC	*Expositor's Bible Commentary*
ECCWE	*Ethnic Chinese Congress on World Evangelization*
FACE	*Completing the Face of the Chinese Church in America: The ABC Handbook Promoting Effective Ministries to American-Born Chinese*
GTJ	*Grace Theological Journal*
ISBE	*The International Standard Bible Encyclopedia*
JETS	*Journal of the Evangelical Theological Society*

JJRS	*Japanese Journal of Religious Studies*
JMT	*The Journal of Ministry & Theology*
NAC	New American Commentary
NICNT	The New International Commentary on the New Testament
NIGTC	New International Greek Testament Commentary
PCNT	Paideia Commentaries on the New Testament
PDTT	*Pocket Dictionary of Theological Terms*
PNTC	The Pillar New Testament Commentary
SANACS	*Society of Asian North American Christian Studies*
TNTC	Tyndale New Testament Commentaries
WBC	Word Biblical Commentary

INTRODUCTION

Established several decades ago, First Church of the Immigrant Believer was one of the first immigrant-language-speaking evangelical churches planted in its host culture. The founding pastor, a first-generation immigrant, began to sense 'the moment of transition' as his children began to grow and attend local public schools. He noticed a trend he had been observing in other immigrant families: his children were becoming assimilated into the host culture, preferring to speak the native language instead of the language of their country of origin and they were starting to view life according to the values, customs, and traditions of this new land in which they were living. Consequently, as his children struggled to form their identity while being torn between these two cultures, they increasingly felt that the church's ministries were culturally irrelevant to them. His children were frustrated because they felt powerless to make any changes since their parents controlled the finances and made the decisions in the church. During this time the pastor wrestled with the difficult options he faced. He could maintain the status quo and inevitably see his children leave for a church in the host culture. Worse still, he could watch them leave the church entirely, probably the most common occurrence among children and grandchildren of other families in his congregation. Or, he could make the necessary and difficult changes to adapt his ministry to the linguistic and cultural needs and preferences of his children and the other children and grandchildren of his immigrant congregation. Torn between what he perceived as a dilemma of keeping his family together or maintaining the status quo, the pastor wrestled with whether he would preserve the language, culture, and traditions of the immigrant generation or make the sacrifices necessary to obediently implement the parallel ministry model of church government in Acts 6:1-7.[1]

Sadly, the dilemma mentioned above is not new, and even more tragic, by failing to deal biblically with the crisis of the immigrant church, wave after wave of immigrants have been futilely repeating the same mistakes of the past two centuries of immigrant church history in the United States. This failure has resulted in the same consequences for each cycle of immigrants regardless of their country of origin:

1. Broken-hearted parents who mourn the loss of relationships with—and the salvation of—their children who leave the culturally irrelevant church.
2. Split, empty, and dying churches which are now filled with grey-haired overseas-born church-people (OBCs) with no one to succeed them in the pulpit and pews.[2]
3. Generations of lost local-born church-people (LBCs), who left a church that failed to meet their needs.
4. A high attrition rate among LBC pastors who are either fired or quit the ministry in bitterness and frustration after only a short period of service because of OBC opposition to their attempts to meet LBC needs.
5. And spiritually immature OBC and LBC congregations and churches that have stagnated due to their failure to live up to

[1] This opening illustration was adapted from Rodriguez's *A Future for the Latino Church* (Daniel A. Rodriguez, *A Future for the Latino Church: Models for Multilingual, Multigenerational Hispanic Congregations*, Kindle ed. [IVP Academic, 2011], Kindle locations 568–582). Hereafter, Kindle locations is abbreviated as "K.l." and Kindle edition books using page numbers appear as "pp./p."

[2] It is uncertain who coined the term OBC, originally referring to "overseas–born Chinese" and adapted to refer to "overseas–born church–people." According to Ling, the term "LBC" was coined by Gail Law in the 1980s to refer to "local–born Chinese" and it is being generalized by this book to refer to "local–born church–people." Samuel Ling and Clarence Cheuk, *The "Chinese" Way of Doing Things: Perspectives on American–Born Chinese and the Chinese Church in North America* (Phillipsburg, NJ: P & R Publishing, 1999), 110. Gail Law, "A Model for the American Ethnic Chinese Churches," in *A Winning Combination: ABC/OBC: Understanding the Cultural Tensions in Chinese Churches*, ed. Cecilia Yau (Petaluma, CA: Chinese Christian Mission, 1986), 131, 141.

> the challenges involved in biblically dealing with the crisis of the immigrant church.[3]

Before another generation of LBCs is lost, before another set of OBC parents are broken hearted, before another immigrant church splits and dies, and before another wave of disillusioned LBC pastors quit, both OBCs and LBCs must rise to the challenge of the crisis of the immigrant church! The challenge will be met not by sociology, by culture, or by copying culturally comfortable solutions that past generations have tried and failed. Rather, the crisis will be solved by following the biblical example of parallel ministry in Acts 6:1-7 so that the whole church, both OBCs and LBCs, may have the chance to grow in number and obedience (Acts 6:7). While the opening narrative about the First Church of the Immigrant Believer may give us some idea of the issues involved, what precisely is the crisis of the immigrant church and how exactly is the crisis solved?

The immigrant church is facing a crisis in which complex cultural and linguistic factors create a reticence on the part of immigrants to transfer financial and decision-making authority to succeeding generations. In turn, this results in a culturally irrelevant ministry to those newer generations, an exodus of believers from the church, a spiritually immature remnant, and an inability to reach the lost.[4] The thesis of this

---

[3] William L. Eng, "Church Programs That Minister Effectively to ABCs," in *FACE* (Oakland, CA: Fellowship of American Chinese Evangelicals (FACE), 2009), 138–44; Joseph C. Wong, "Culturally–Sensitive OBC Leadership," in *FACE* (Oakland, CA: Fellowship of American Chinese Evangelicals (FACE), 2009), 97–100.

[4] Although the term "exodus" was used much earlier (FACE 1990), according to Chan, Kang, and Hackman, the phrase "silent exodus" was coined by Helen Lee in her article by that name to describe the flight of LBC Asians from the OBC church. Popularly, the phrase refers to the fact that, due to their non–confrontational culture, LBC Asians may not complain and will simply leave "silently." Others such as Phillips use the term "second generation exodus" or just "exodus" to describe the same phenomena in other ethnic groups. Cecilia C. Chan, "Where Have the Children Gone?: Young Adult Commitment in Chinese Protestant Churches in United States" (D.M. diss., Case Western Reserve University, Cleveland, OH, 2007), 4; S. Steve Kang and Megan A. Hackman, "Toward a Broader Role in Mission: How Korean Americans' Struggle for Identity Can Lead to a Renewed Vision for Mission," *International Bulletin for Missionary Research* April 36, no. 2 (2012): 76; Helen Lee, "Silent Exodus: Can the East Asian Church in America Reverse the Flight of Its Next Generation?,"

book is that parallel ministry, based on Acts 6:1-7, is the biblical solution to the crisis in the immigrant church. The immigrant church may be facing other problems, some particular to the diverse cultures of various ethnic groups, but the persistent problem that all immigrant groups face and historically have failed to deal with successfully is that of effectively reaching the next generations. Consequently, the issue of effectively reaching the next generations is one of, if not the greatest problem facing the immigrant church as a whole and may be accurately described as "the crisis" of the immigrant church. There are at least two main aspects of this crisis: a spiritual-relational and an ecclesiastical aspect.

The spiritual-relational aspect involves a whole host of issues, such as changed attitudes that are not the primary concern of this book, but must be implemented in conjunction with the ecclesiastical solution in order for either aspect of the solution to be successful. Some spiritual-relational issues include the raising awareness of specific cultural differences between immigrants and succeeding generations in order to improve communication, recognizing and changing particular attitudes and values of immigrants and succeeding generations, examining how leaders from the succeeding generations are identified and trained both in the church and by seminaries, and describing what culturally relevant worship, preaching, leadership, and philosophy of ministry styles look like. Another frequently discussed spiritual–relational issue is the identification of "bridge people" or bilingual–bicultural individuals (people typically, but not necessarily from the 1.5 generation) who are able to facilitate communication and understanding between OBCs and LBCs. (The 1.5 generation refers to those LBCs who were "born abroad but raised primarily in the United States" and the second generation refers to those LBCs who were "born in the United States to foreign–born parents.")[5] Perhaps the best discussion of the spiritual-relational aspect to date is found in chapter 9 of Ling's *The "Chinese" Way of Doing Things*.[6] Although Ling writes from a Chinese perspective, it is likely that much of

---

Christianity Today 40, no. 9 (1996): 50; Mercidieu Phillips, "Resolving the Causes of Second Generation Exodus from the Haitian Church in South Florida" (D.Ed.Min. diss., Bethel Seminary, Saint Paul, MN, 2011), 6; Joseph C. Wong, "Culturally–Sensitive," 77–78.

[5] Alex Stepick and Carol Dutton Stepick, "Becoming American, Constructing Ethnicity: Immigrant Youth and Civic Engagement," *Applied Developmental Science* 6, no. 4 (2002): 248.

[6] Ling and Cheuk, *Chinese Way*, 135–60.

his cultural analysis has parallels in other immigrant cultures. Moreover, Ling's work serves as a model for how to think through the spiritual-relational issues for other ethnic immigrant groups and on how to go about implementing parallel ministry. However, the ecclesiastical aspect of the crisis is the main concern of *Solving the Immigrant Church Crisis*.

The ecclesiastical aspect, by definition, concerns how the immigrant church should be organizationally structured. The term "ecclesiology" is derived from the Greek word for "church" [ἐκκλησία] and is that "branch of systematic theology that treats the church, covering such things as the scriptural definition of its names, nature, government, and power."[7] "Ecclesiology seeks to set forth the nature and function of the church. It also investigates issues such as the mission, ministry and structure of the church."[8] Consequently, the ecclesiastical aspect of the crisis involves setting forth the biblical evidence for how the immigrant church is to be structured. The present ecclesiological proposal is that Acts 6:1-7 defines parallel ministry as entailing interdependent (Acts 6:7) and culturally relevant ministries to OBCs and LBCs (Acts 6:1), each with their own financial (Acts 6:2) and decision-making authority (Acts 6:3-6). This book uses the phrase, "*The* Biblical Solution," in its title because the following chapters will argue that Acts 6:1-7 is the biblical passage that most directly relates to the crisis of the immigrant church by setting forth an explicit example of church structure and government applicable to the immigrant church.

This book will demonstrate that, according to Acts 6:1-7, the ecclesiastical parallel ministry structure exists when favorable spiritual-relational conditions occur in such a way that OBCs transfer financial and decision-making authority to LBCs so that they may create a culturally relevant interdependent ministry that allows for the needs of both groups to be met. In this interpretation of Acts 6:1-7, the passage explicitly and implicitly states that the parallel ministry ecclesiastical structure consists,

---

[7] Alan Cairns, *DTT* (Greenville, SC: Ambassador Emerald International, 2002), in *Logos Library System* [CD–ROM], s.v. "Ecclesiology."

[8] Stanley Grenz, David Guretzki, and Cherith Fee Nordling, *PDTT* (Downers Grove: InterVarsity, 1999), in *Logos Library System* [*CD–ROM*], s.v. "ecclesiology."

not only of separate and culturally relevant OBC and LBC worship services, but also co-pastors and different offerings, budgets, boards, and visions that are part of a single interdependent church. The various elements that make up the structure are "parallel," because while OBCs and LBCs each have their separate respective ecclesiastical components, those components are interdependent rather than independent or dependent upon each other. To gain a further initial understanding of the parallel ministry structure, please see Figures 1 and 2 and Tables 1 and 3 in the lists of illustrations and tables.

The remainder of this book will explain how this structure solves the crisis of the immigrant church, why it is the biblical solution to the crisis, how this structure is derived from Acts 6:1-7, and why the alternatives to parallel ministry are deficient solutions to the crisis. These alternatives to parallel ministry include bilingual worship, separate worship services, and church planting. Bilingual worship involves using some type of translation between the OBC and LBC languages, typically only in a worship service. Separate services involve different worship services for OBCs and LBCs that meet at different times and/or locations. Church planting seeks to plant LBC churches that are independent from OBC churches.

While most works treating this crisis deal with both the spiritual-relational as well as the ecclesiastical aspects, this book focuses on the ecclesiastical aspect, because the majority of past proposals effectively describe the spiritual-relational aspect from a sociological perspective, but do not provide an ecclesiastical solution with a sufficient biblical basis. This book argues that the plethora of previous solutions are all deficient, because they have an insufficient biblical basis. Some of the proposals are deficient because they only describe rather than solve the problem (Ling, Zaki), compromise their biblical basis with sociological-cultural qualifications (Ethnic Chinese Congress on World Evangelization [ECCWE], Fellowship of American Chinese Evangelicals [FACE], Ortiz, Phillips, Rodriguez), or combine a sociological-cultural basis with a counterproductive solution (Fong, Jeung, Pai).[9]

---

[9] Sharon Wai–Man Chan, ed. *ECCWE* (Tsim Sha Tsui, Hong Kong: Chinese Coordination Centre of World Evangelism, 1986); William L. Eng and others, *FACE* (Oakland, CA: Fellowship of American Chinese Evangelicals [FACE], 2009); Ken Uyeda Fong, *Pursuing the Pearl: A Comprehensive Resource for Multi–Asian Ministry*, Updated ed. (Valley Forge, PA: Judson Press, 1999); Russell Jeung, *Faithful Generations: Race and New Asian American Churches*, Kindle ed. (New Brunswick, NJ: Rutgers University Press, 2005); Ling and Cheuk, *Chinese Way*; Manuel Ortiz, *The*

The thesis is defended through a problem-solution format in which the crisis of the immigrant church is described (chapter 1), the present proposal is offered (chapters 2-3), and the deficiencies of previous solutions are explained (chapters 4-5). Chapter 1 argues that the crisis of the immigrant church is a universal experience common to all ethnic groups in the immigration history of the United States. As evidence of the universal nature and as a description of the crisis, the observations of sociological studies from different ethnic standpoints are compiled into a synthetic whole that represents the common experience of several diverse immigrant groups. A section containing personal correspondence with both OBCs and LBCs in immigrant churches illustrates some of the points raised in the sociological studies.

Chapter 2 introduces the parallel ministry ecclesiastical structure by demonstrating how it is derived from a detailed exegesis of Act 6:1-7. The exegesis is conducted in two parts: the first part handles the explicit meaning of the passage and the second part deals with some implications. A normative definition of parallel ministry is constructed from the conclusions of the exegesis. Some of the points of the definition receive further explanation.

Chapter 3 summarizes the conclusions of the exegesis from chapter 2, argues for the unique and normative nature of the proposal, and evaluates the parallel ministry model through an objection and response format.

In chapter 4, the three past proposed solutions are introduced and described: the bilingual worship, separate worship services, and church planting models. These three models are strung together as phases in a typical cycle of immigrant church growth. A description of the state of the church according to several uniform criteria is provided for each stage of growth/model.

Hispanic Challenge: Opportunities Confronting the Church (Downers Grove: InterVarsity, 1993); Hyo Shick Pai, "Korean Congregational Church of Los Angeles: The Bilingual Ministry and Its Impact on Church Growth" (D.Ed.Min. diss., Fuller Theological Seminary, Pasadena, CA, 1987); Phillips, "Haitian Church"; Rodriguez, *Latino Church*; Zaki Labib Zaki, "'How Shall We Sing the Lord's Song in a New Land?': A Survey of the Needs and Challenges Facing the Educational Ministry of the Middle Eastern American Church" (D.Ed.Min. diss., Chicago Theological Seminary, Chicago, IL, 1998).

In chapter 5, the proposals for each model made by specific historical figures are introduced and evaluated: bilingual (Pai), separate service (*FACE Handbook*), and church planting (Fong).[10] Furthermore, each model is evaluated based on its individual merits apart from the historic proposals.

While this book develops an argument progressively through the five chapters that make up its main body so that reading it cover to cover may provide the most benefit, it need not be read sequentially from cover to cover. The simple problem-solution structure is intended to accommodate a variety of readers.

This book strives to make both an academic and a practical contribution. Academically, this book offers a model for the proper Christian method of solving the church's ecclesiological issues through a scriptural solution, whereas sociology only provides a description of the problem. Some may think that sociology provides a valid basis for ecclesiological solutions and/or other theological endeavors. However, for evangelicals, there are only three types of arguments: biblically based, biblically consistent, and biblically inconsistent.

Biblically based arguments begin with Scripture and argue their case from specific biblical passages.

Biblically consistent arguments may use broad biblical themes, images, symbols or other biblical elements, or extra-biblical sources, such as sociology or philosophy as a starting point or as the mechanism to formulate their argument, but the concepts presented are consistent with and do not contradict the Bible. In practice, biblical consistency is often not explicitly shown. However, since many arguments that assume biblical consistency are actually biblically inconsistent, then as a safeguard against error, it is prudent to explicitly demonstrate concord with the biblical text.

Biblically inconsistent arguments are those that may assume consistency, but either as a whole or in parts contradict the Bible. Biblical inconsistency sometimes occurs when authors misinterpret the Bible. It more frequently occurs when authors begin with a non-biblical starting point, such as sociology or culture, and assume consistency. (The sociological elements involved in the arguments surrounding the crisis of the immigrant church may include, but are not limited to, culture, case study approaches, demographic studies, contemporary missiology, or church growth principles.) In this case, authors will frequently veer away from the Bible as their argument develops because they merely express

---

[10] Eng, *FACE*; Fong, *Multi–Asian Ministry*; Pai, "Bilingual Ministry."

their opinion or because they unknowingly accept extra-biblical presuppositions, data, or other factors in their extra-biblical source that contradict the Bible. Even if an ecclesiological solution attempts to provide a biblically consistent sociological basis, the Bible must be the ultimate foundation underlying the solution or else the argument is biblically inconsistent.

The Bible, rather than sociology, must be the basis of an ecclesiological solution. The reformation doctrine of *sola Scriptura* [Scripture alone] includes the doctrine of the sufficiency of Scripture. The sufficiency of Scripture is the idea that Scripture "contains everything we need God to tell us for salvation, for trusting him perfectly, and for obeying him perfectly…the Bible is sufficient to equip us for living the Christian life (Tim. 3:16-17)."[11] The doctrine of sufficiency and its basis in 2 Timothy 3:16-17 have been hotly debated in the history of theology.[12] Since sociology frequently contradicts the Bible, then whatever 2 Timothy 3:16-17 and its interpretation in the doctrine of sufficiency may mean, sufficiency entails the idea that the Bible, rather than sociology, provides normative direction on how the church should structure itself. The Bible, not sociology, is the final authority or "the rule of faith and life" for believers and must provide the solution to the crisis of the immigrant church.[13]

In general, biblically based arguments are better than biblically consistent arguments, because their biblical starting point and explicit biblical connection guards against violations of the doctrine of sufficiency and against inconsistencies introduced from extra-biblical starting points and the unreliability of human opinion. The past proposals examined by this book provide deficient biblical support in at least one of several ways: not being biblically based, falsely assuming or insufficiently demonstrating biblical consistency, or being biblically inconsistent. In

---

[11] Emphasis removed. Wayne A. Grudem, *Systematic Theology: An Introduction to Biblical Doctrine* (Grand Rapids: InterVarsity; Zondervan, 2004), in *Logos Library System* [CD–ROM], 127.

[12] Keith A. Mathison, *The Shape of Sola Scriptura* (Moscow, ID: Canon, 2001), 163.

[13] Westminster Assembly, *The Westminster Confession of Faith* (Oak Harbor, WA: Logos Research Systems, 1996), in *Logos Library System* [CD–ROM], s.v. "Chapter 1, Section 2."

some cases, the biblical inconsistency may involve faulty extra-biblical presuppositions which result in faulty interpretation. In other proposals, there is a failure to establish a valid analogy between the biblical text and the crisis of the immigrant church in the process of application or solution. The proposal offered by this book attempts to provide a biblically based solution involving a valid analogy between the text and the crisis.

Practically, this book offers a specific biblical solution to an actual problem that numerous immigrant churches around the world are currently facing. While the biblical-ecclesiological solution of parallel ministry proposed by this book is not new, part of what is new is its universal focus on all immigrant groups and its foundation on the Bible rather than sociology and culture, which gives the solution an ethically normative basis appropriate to the universal nature of the crisis.

While the church will want to act wisely, there is also a practical need to act quickly. By the time most immigrant churches recognize the need to care for the spiritual needs of their children and pick up a book like this to address the situation, it may be already too late. It takes time for a church to decide to implement parallel ministry and once it does, it must find and hire, at minimum, an LBC youth pastor and ideally an LBC pastor, youth pastor, and children's minister. All of this process may take at least two to four years or more for immigrant groups that make decisions based on consensus. Once the pastoral staff is in place and other structural changes such as parallel worship services and fellowships are established, it may take at least another two to three years for the new structure to make a lasting impact on LBCs. If the church already has LBCs in junior and senior high, then some of them may graduate and leave the church for good before a relevant ministry is even established for them.[14]

While children need a good spiritual foundation in the children's ministry, there is only a seven-year critical window of opportunity in junior and senior high before they leave for college. During this window, they need to be grounded in the faith and to recognize that there is or will be a culturally relevant ministry for them to return to after they graduate. This seven-year window is critical, because once children go to college, whether they physically leave their parents or not, they are adults who cannot be forced to attend a church, particularly if it is not culturally relevant to them. Furthermore, they will not attend any church if

[14] For a similar judgment see: Wong, "Culturally–Sensitive," 97–100.

they were not grounded in their faith during their youth. Although many have a spiritual experience in college as a result of parachurch campus fellowship groups, historically, many more do not demonstrate a true and lasting faith after graduation and fall away if they were not grounded earlier and/or have a relevant church to return to after graduation. Many, if not most, immigrant churches currently do not have a significant young adult LBC ministry in large part because most left the church after college due to its cultural irrelevance and failure to meet their needs. Youth and college graduates leave or never attend a church due to a number of factors. For example, many students move to another area for college, find a job there, and so never return to their home church. However, for immigrant churches, a major, if not the major, reason why youth and young adults leave their church is due to its cultural irrelevance and failure to meet their needs. Please read this book carefully, but quickly, to learn about the practical solution of parallel ministry in Acts 6:1-7 and implement it with haste and careful discernment.

It is time to stop repeating the mistakes of past generations of immigrants and reaping the same consequences of their mistakes. It is insufficient to ignore the problems of the immigrant church or to merely look to other failed or failing immigrant churches for solutions as many OBC do to solve the problem. A biblical solution is needed. A practical solution is needed. A successful solution is needed. The parallel ministry of Acts 6:1-7 must be implemented not only to stop the silent exodus so that LBCs will not fall away and not only to preserve immigrant churches and prevent OBC hearts from breaking, but also so that both OBCs and LBCs may reach spiritual maturity and unity in Christ (Eph. 4:2-6, 13, 16).

CHAPTER 1. Problem Description

At the end of my three-month short term mission trip to Japan, our team reassembled for a debriefing retreat after having served alone in separate churches for the majority of the trip. At the highpoint of the retreat, the night before we returned home, the team split up into groups of three to present skits representing something they learned or something of their experience in Japan. One group decided to present their skit in almost total silence, just acting out their story through universal hand gestures and facial expressions so that the audience of missionaries and Japanese nationals could understand.

As their skit began, they finished a breakfast served by one of the nationals who was pretending to be their host mother, packed their bags, pretended to leave the house, and sat on a bench very methodically putting on and tying their shoes. Then they acted as if they had walked quite a distance. Suddenly, one of them stopped, turned to the audience and looked shocked. Frantically, they rummaged through their backpack looking for something, slowly placing numerous contents on the stage for everyone to see. They gestured among themselves that they had forgotten something. Slowly, the three of them repacked the bag, pretended to walk back to the host home, and methodically took off their shoes. They went back into the house and got a Bible. Then they methodically put on and tied their shoes and pretended to walk a long distance. Again, one of them stopped, looked shocked, unpacked their bag, and then returned to the host home, first methodically taking off their shoes before entering to retrieve their forgotten item. Then they left the house and hastily put back on their shoes, looking somewhat frustrated.

They repeated this pattern a few more times, each time taking off and putting on their shoes more quickly and looking more frustrated. On the final trip back to the host home to retrieve a forgotten item, the three missionaries gave each other looks of exasperation outside the imaginary front door of the house. They then slowly pretended to open it, looked around to see that no one was there, and slowly tiptoed into the house without having taken off their shoes. Exploding on stage from the kitchen and shouting in Japanese, the national who was pretending to be their host mother, pointed at their shoes with one hand, while chasing them out of the house with a broom in the other hand. The audience burst into laughter.

When one lives in a particular culture, the social conventions are, as Fong has compared, like the air one breathes or the water in which a fish swims.[1] The social conventions are constantly around us, but we seldom notice them. However, when we come into contact with another culture and its social conventions, such as taking our shoes off before entering the house, the social customs of the other culture may become restrictive, and one may feel like there is smoke in the air that makes it difficult to breathe or like a freshwater fish dumped in saltwater.

And herein lies a major part of the problem of the crisis of the immigrant church: like the missionaries in the skit, LBCs get frustrated with taking their shoes off and on for OBCs, and like the host mother, OBCs get frustrated with LBCs who want to wear their shoes in the church. This clash of cultures is a universal experience that is not unique to any one ethnic or immigrant group when encountering another culture. The nature and intensity of the clash may vary somewhat depending on the different social customs and other factors, but the reality of the clash remains basically the same.

The crisis of the immigrant church is a problem that generally is common to all immigrants. However, this book is primarily concerned with immigrants in the United States and within the evangelical Christian tradition. The immigrant church in the U.S. is the primary focus, because

---

[1] Ken Uyeda Fong, *Pursuing the Pearl: A Comprehensive Resource for Multi–Asian Ministry*, Updated ed. (Valley Forge, PA: Judson Press, 1999), 21, 194.

it seems that, to date, no other country in the world has experienced as much and as diverse immigration as the U.S.[2] The history of immigration in the U.S. conventionally is divided into two main stages by the Immigration Act of 1965, which reversed the immigration exclusion acts of the 1920s.[3] In the first stage and prior to 1965, immigration to the U.S. was primarily from Europe and Africa and, to a much lesser extent, Asia, but in the second stage after 1965, immigrants came from Asia, the Middle East, Mexico, South-Central America, and the Caribbean.[4]

Among the religions of these immigrants, Evangelical Christianity is highlighted, because it is the faith tradition from within which this book is written. However, it is likely that many of the claims made by this book are relevant not only to evangelical immigrant churches in other countries, but also those of various Christian traditions and other religions which have a congregational ecclesiastical structure. For example, Sullivan's study, "Catherine's Catholic Church: One Church, Parallel Congregations," describes a specific Catholic church, consisting of immigrants from Asia, the Middle East, Mexico, South–Central America, and the Caribbean, as having the same crisis in which cultural irrelevance in part due to language and reluctance to transfer financial and decision–making power is causing the succeeding generations to leave the church.[5]

---

[2] D. Mauk and J. Oakland, *American Civilization: An Introduction*, Reprint ed. (New York: Routledge, 2005), 67; Organization for Economic Co-operation and Development [OECD], *A Profile of Immigrant Populations in the 21st Century: Data from OECD Countries* (Danvers, MA: OECD Publishing, 2008), 14, 16; Dilip Ratha, Sanket Mohapatra, and Ani Silwal, *Migration and Remittances Factbook 2011*, 2nd ed. (Washngton D.C.: The World Bank, 2011), ix, 1. For a similar judgment see: Ronald H. Bayor, "Series Foreword," in *The Chinese Americans* of The New Americans, ed. Ronald H. Bayor (Westport, CT: Greenwood, 2000), ix.

[3] Bayor, "Series Foreword," ix; Shelley Sang–Hee Lee, *A New History of Asian America*, (New York: Routledge, 2014), 121, 317; R. Stephen Warner, "Introduction: Immigration and Religious Communities in the United States," in *Gatherings in Diaspora: Religious Communities and the New Immigration*, Kindle ed., R. Stephen Warner and Judith G. Wittner eds. (Philadelphia: Temple University Press, 1998), K.l. 56–57, 67–70.

[4] Bayor, "Series Foreword," ix; ; Sucheng Chan, *Asian Americans: An Interpretive History*, ed. Thomas J. Archdeacon, Revised and Updated ed., Twayne's Immigrant Heritage of America (Boston: Twayne, 1991), 145; Lee, *New History*, 121, 317; Warner, "Introduction," 27–32.

[5] Kathleen Sullivan, "Catherine's Catholic Church: One Church, Parallel Congregations," in *Religion and the New Immigrants: Continuities and Adaptations*, Kindle ed., Helen

While Jeung and others dispute the universal nature of the immigrant crisis, Warner's analysis of Niebuhr's description of pre-1965 immigrant problems is essentially correct: there is a "continuity of the immigrant religious experience between the nineteenth century and the present."[6] The claim that there is general continuity in the crisis of the immigrant church does not mean that there are no specific cultural or other differences between pre-1965 and post-1965 immigrants or between groups or individuals within either period, but rather that the general

---

Rose Ebaugh and Janet Saltzman Chafetz eds. (Walnut Creek, CA: Altamira Press, 2000), pp. 255, 260. On the universal nature of the problem among American immigrants also see: Fong, *Multi–Asian Ministry*, 194; Manuel Ortiz, *The Hispanic Challenge: Opportunities Confronting the Church* (Downers Grove: InterVarsity, 1993), 19, 85–87. Sources that indicate the crisis is a universal problem for all immigrants around the world include: Sharon Wai–Man Chan, ed. *ECCWE* (Tsim Sha Tsui, Hong Kong: Chinese Coordination Centre of World Evangelism, 1986), 65–68, 107–08, 127–29, 138–40, 143–64; Samuel Ling and Clarence Cheuk, *The "Chinese" Way of Doing Things: Perspectives on American–Born Chinese and the Chinese Church in North America* (Phillipsburg, NJ: P&R, 1999), 109–18, 187, 203–04, 206. With regard to other religions see: Pyong Gap Min, *Preserving Ethnicity through Religion in America: Korean Protestants and Indian Hindus across Generations*, Kindle ed. (New York: New York University Press, 2010), K.l. 411–16, 427–29, 439–42; Mark Mullins, "The Life Cycle of Ethnic Churches in Sociological Perspective," *JJRS* 14, no. 4 (1987): 328–30.

[6] Warner, "Introduction," K.l. 167–70. Warner indicates that several of the other contributors to his multi–author work hold that the experiences of racial discrimination and "transnationalism" (lack of assimilation due to contact with one's home country) differ between pre and post 1965 immigrants Ibid., 170–89. Jeung cites a number of scholars who also hold to a difference in experience based on racial discrimination. Russell Jeung, *Faithful Generations: Race and New Asian American Churches*, Kindle ed. [New Brunswick, NJ: Rutgers University Press, 2005), K.l. 188–94. Mullins not only agrees with Warner's analysis of Niebuhr, but also gives multiple Canadian examples of the universal nature of the problem among various immigrant groups. Mullins, "Ethnic Churches," 322–25, 328–30. For a similar judgment see: Kenneth P. Carlson, "Patterns in Development of the English Ministry in a Chinese Church," in *The 2008 Report: The Bay Area Chinese Churches Research Project Phase II*, ed. James Chuck and Timothy Tseng (Castro Valley, CA: The Institute for the Study of Asian American Christianity, 2009), 207, 212; Manuel Ortiz, "Foreword," in *A Future for the Latino Church: Models for Multilingual, Multigenerational Hispanic Congregations* (IVP Academic, 2011), 47–51; Ortiz, *Hispanic Challenge*, 19.

problem is basically the same.[7] For example, when Niebuhr claims, regarding pre-1965 immigrants, that the "histories of most other foreign-language immigrant churches repeat these conflicts between the language parties in the church … the parties came into conflict in many local churches and frequently divided into two separate congregations … by the defection of youth to American ways and to the English language," he describes the same basic problem depicted in contemporary studies on the crisis in the post-1965 immigrant church.[8]

There is a threefold significance of the universality of the crisis of the immigrant church: methodological, theological, and practical. Methodologically, the universal nature of the crisis means that the various sources depicting the problem from the perspective of different ethnic groups may be drawn upon to discuss the problem in a general manner.

Theologically, the fact that the problem is universal and crosses cultural lines suggests that it is a problem of sin at its root, and particularly, but not exclusively, it is the sin of pride which impacts all people regardless of ethnicity (Eccl. 7:20; Rom. 6:23; 1 Cor. 10:13).[9] The problem of immigrant ministry is basically a problem of sin hindering God's work. The OBC desire of wanting to preserve one's language and culture is not an inherently sinful desire, but when it begins to hinder effective ministry to others, then pride causes this desire to become an idol in the sense that such preservation becomes more important than God's

---

[7] For a similar judgment see: Mullins, "Ethnic Churches," 330–31; Ortiz, "Foreword," 60–61; Mercidieu Phillips, "Resolving the Causes of Second Generation Exodus from the Haitian Church in South Florida" (D.Ed.Min. diss., Bethel Seminary, Saint Paul, MN, 2011), 80.

[8] H. Richard Niebuhr, *The Social Sources of Denominationalism* (Hamden, CT: H. Holt and Company, 1929, reprint, 1954), 227, 229. For contemporary studies that provide a similar problem description see: William L. Eng and others, *FACE* (Oakland, CA: Fellowship of American Chinese Evangelicals [FACE], 2009), 7, 18, 21, 70, 78; Jeung, *Faithful Generations*, K.l. 890–904; Min, *Korean Protestants*, K.l. 1788–91, 2889–92, 4231–34, 5244–46; Phillips, "Haitian Church," 4, 94, 134–38; Daniel A. Rodriguez, *A Future for the Latino Church: Models for Multilingual, Multigenerational Hispanic Congregations*, Kindle ed. (IVP Academic, 2011), K.l. 129–131, 639–43; Zaki Labib Zaki, "'How Shall We Sing the Lord's Song in a New Land?': A Survey of the Needs and Challenges Facing the Educational Ministry of the Middle Eastern American Church" (D.Ed.Min. diss., Chicago Theological Seminary, Chicago, IL, 1998), 6, 17, 28.

[9] For a similar judgment see: William L. Eng, "An Overview of Christian Work among ABCs," in *FACE* (Oakland, CA: FACE, 2009), 72; Ling and Cheuk, *Chinese Way*, 136; Phillips, "Haitian Church," 126–27.

purposes and service. At the same time, LBC pride in assuming cultural superiority when communicating their needs to OBCs hinders the communication process. In resolving this crisis, humility is required of all (James 4:6). Certainly this claim that sin is the root of the problem is very significant and deserves additional discussion, but it is part of the spiritual–relational aspect of the problem and further comment is out of the scope of this study.

Practically, the universal nature of the problem means that present immigrants should learn from the immigrants of the past so as not to make the same mistakes. Furthermore, the theological-ethical nature of the problem means that the practical application of the biblical solution applies universally.

A Picture from Past Sociological Studies

The general crisis of the immigrant church is that it universally and historically has not provided a culturally relevant ministry to succeeding generations due in part to a reticence to transfer financial and decision-making authority. However, there are a number of specific and universal cultural and linguistic factors that contribute to the crisis. In order to depict the specifics of the universal crisis of the immigrant church, other studies provide detailed sociological descriptions of particular cultural differences between OBCs and LBCs in individual ethnic groups. Among these OBC-LBC differences, there are a number of common concerns shared by OBCs and LBCs respectively in many different cultures. By listing these respective concerns, a picture is painted of how OBC ministry fails to be biblically based and culturally relevant or to meet the needs of LBCs. The picture also demonstrates why it is necessary, but OBCs are reticent to transfer financial and decision-making authority to LBCs in order for the needs of both groups to be met. The remainder of this chapter describes first the common concerns relating to the problem of cultural relevance and then the concerns relating to the transfer of financial and decision-making power.

A difference in cultural concerns between OBCs and LBCs results in a culturally irrelevant ministry in the minds of LBCs and culminates in their exodus from the OBC church. OBCs typically are concerned with trying to preserve their language and culture by passing them on to the next generations so that the language used, styles of attire, music, worship, preaching, leadership, philosophy of ministry, and vision are all shaped by this concern.[10] In contrast, 1.5 and second generation LBCs usually face an identity crisis in which they simultaneously identify with and are alienated by both the host and OBC cultures while developing their own unique subculture at the same time.[11] Due to the cultural and linguistic differences, the OBC ministry is culturally irrelevant to the LBCs and so fails to meet their spiritual and other needs.[12] Consequently, the silent or second generation exodus occurs in which the majority of LBCs usually leave the OBC church once they are old enough to do so.[13] While some LBCs will attend host culture churches, most LBCs are not completely comfortable with the host culture and so remain unchurched and often unsaved.[14] LBC churches are also becoming more

---

[10] Helen Lee, "Silent Exodus: Can the East Asian Church in America Reverse the Flight of Its Next Generation?," *Christianity Today* 40, no. 9 (1996): 50; Min, *Korean Protestants*, K.l. 1769, 1782–84; Mullins, "Ethnic Churches," 322; Phillips, "Haitian Church," 102–03; Rodriguez, *Latino Church*, K.l. 129–31, 174–76, 568–72, 718–21; David K. Woo, "Power for Future ABC Ministries," in *FACE* (Oakland, CA: FACE, 2009), 180; Zaki, "Middle Eastern American Church," 6, 17, 28.

[11] Fabienne Doucet and Carola Suarez–Orozco, "Ethnic Identity and Schooling the Experiences of Haitian Immigrant Youth," in *Ethnic Identity: Problems and Prospects for the Twenty–First Century*, 4th, Kindle ed. Lola Romanucci–Ross, De George A. Vos, and Takeyuki Tsuda eds. (New York: Alta Mira Press, 2006), K.l. 3476–78; Lee, "Silent Exodus," 53; Min, *Korean Protestants*, K.l. 660–65; Ortiz, *Hispanic Challenge*, 81, 85, 87; Phillips, "Haitian Church," 74–75, 78, 125, 129; Rodriguez, *Latino Church*, K.l. 141–49, 926–28, 1275–77; Wayland Wong, "Who Are the American–Born Chinese?," in *FACE* (Oakland, CA: FACE, 2009), 29–30; Zaki, "Middle Eastern American Church," 19.

[12] William L. Eng, "Church Programs That Minister Effectively to ABCs," in *FACE* (Oakland, CA: FACE, 2009), 140; Lee, "Silent Exodus," 50; Min, *Korean Protestants*, K.l. 3182–96; Phillips, "Haitian Church," 103, 106–07, 110–11, 122–23; Rodriguez, *Latino Church*, K.l. 118–19, 129–31, 728–32, 1551.

[13] Moses Chow and David T. Chow, "Practical Cooperation Programs and Projects between Overseas–Born Chinese and Local–Born Chinese," in *ECCWE*, ed. Sharon Wai–Man Chan (Tsim Sha Tsui, Hong Kong: Chinese Coordination Centre of World Evangelism, 1986), 152; Eng, *FACE*, 5, 8, 77–78, 170; Ling and Cheuk, *Chinese Way*, 145; Min, *Korean Protestants*, K.l. 669–75, 2889–92, 4231–34; Mullins, "Ethnic Churches," 326; Ortiz, *Hispanic Challenge*, 122; Phillips, "Haitian Church," 95–96, 106–07; Rodriguez, *Latino Church*, K.l. 572–82.

[14] Eng, "Overview," 70–71; Lee, "Silent Exodus," 52; Jeung, *Faithful Generations*, K.l. 734–35, 748–49, 848–50, 853–54; Min, *Korean Protestants*, K.l. 714–16, 3221–22; Phillips, "Haitian Church," 13–14; Rodriguez, *Latino Church*, K.l. 139–41, 639–43;Wong, "American–Born Chinese," 32.

prevalent, and their impact on the exodus is discussed in the objection and response section in chapter 3 and the section dealing with the church planting model in chapter 5.

Although many OBCs are aware of the second generation exodus, in addition to other factors, the "illusion of success" makes it difficult for them to effectively address the problem.[15] The "illusion of success" takes at least two forms. First, as long as immigration from the OBC home country continues, the pews vacated by LBCs are continuously filled and the OBC congregation grows despite LBC losses. Consequently, the loss of LBCs is not immediately apparent, thus giving the illusion of success.[16] Second, even when LBC ministries are established within the OBC church, the ecclesiastical organization is typically such that the ministry structure fails to meet the needs of *both* LBCs and OBCs. Since the various organizational structures meet some of the needs of each group, then the satisfaction felt by meeting some of the needs gives the illusion of success, which conceals the fact that other needs of each group are unmet.

There are two additional problems related to the illusion of success. First, immigrants from past waves of immigration typically do not communicate with immigrants from the current wave. A variety of practical and cultural factors contribute to a lack of communication between immigrants of different immigration periods. For example, past generations of immigrants may be deceased by the time new immigrants arrive, their churches may have closed by the time the new immigrants arrive, or the immigrants may be from different cultural or ethnic groups. Whatever the reasons, the lack of communication between past and current immigrants results in the current immigrants having an illusion of success, when in fact past groups would warn current groups that they have already tried their methods and failed. Second, every time a new

---

[15] On OBC awareness see: William L. Eng, "Having an Effective Model for ABC Ministry within the Chinese Church," in *FACE* (Oakland, CA: Fellowship of American Chinese Evangelicals (FACE), 2009), 111; Phillips, "Haitian Church," 105, 116, 118–20; Rodriguez, *Latino Church*, K.l. 583–86. The *FACE Handbook* does not use the term "illusion of success," but it has the concept. Wong, "American–Born Chinese," 32.

[16] Ibid., 32.

wave of immigration occurs, LBC leaders are faced with the daunting task of reeducating the OBC newcomers about the crisis of the immigrant church and parallel ministry. In some cases, LBC leaders who have been working with OBC leadership for years to move toward parallel ministry have their work set back a decade or more by new immigrants who take positions of leadership either on the board or the pastoral staff of OBC churches. Once parallel ministry is established, the burden of education falls more to the OBC than LBC leaders, dramatically reducing LBC pastoral burnout and church tensions.

A difference in cultural concerns between OBCs and LBCs results in the reticence of OBCs to transfer financial and decision-making authority to LBCs. In turn, this culminates in the LBC exodus from the OBC church. OBCs typically hold the financial and decision-making power in immigrant churches because they tend to be the parents of the LBC members.[17] Several OBC and LBC concerns contribute to the OBCs' reticence to transfer financial and decision-making power:

First, at earlier stages in congregational development, no LBCs may be old enough financially to support and lead the LBC ministry, and OBCs may be reluctant to trust outsiders from the host culture to help with the LBC ministry.[18]

Second, OBC staff may fear that they will become unnecessary and be replaced by bilingual LBC leaders.[19] Lowe points out that while numerical growth is valued by both OBCs and LBCs, OBCs feel threatened by large LBC congregations. Consequently, this fear may contribute to OBC reticence to transfer financial and decision–making authority.[20] LBCs often are afraid to shed the security of OBC ministry and risk the financial and other responsibilities involved in parallel ministry.[21]

---

[17] Joseph C. Wong, "Culturally–Sensitive OBC Leadership," in *FACE* (Oakland, CA: Fellowship of American Chinese Evangelicals (FACE), 2009), 94.

[18] Phillips, "Haitian Church," 118; Min, *Korean Protestants*, K.l. 669–75.

[19] Phillips, "Haitian Church," 142; Ortiz, *Hispanic Challenge*, 83; Wong, "American–Born Chinese," 48. For a similar fear among laypeople see: Rodriguez, *Latino Church*, K.l. 683–84. Also see a general comment on immigrant fears of "giving up control": Jeung, *Faithful Generations*, K.l. 2251–52.

[20] Curtis Lowe to Ronald M. Rothenberg, "Discussion of Parallel Ministry," 25 October 2014, FaceTime.

[21] Lowe, "Discussion," FaceTime.

Third, OBC lay leaders may be men who have lost the professional and political prestige they held in their home country and have replaced that status with their leadership position in the church.[22] They may feel reluctant to relinquish even a portion of the prestige they have recovered through their church leadership position. Consequently, LBCs who wish to have shared ownership of the church often feel disenfranchised.[23] The next two concerns of OBCs likely contribute more than any other factors to OBCs' reticence to transfer financial and decision-making authority.

Fourth, OBCs usually have a different cultural understanding of spiritual maturity than LBCs.[24] As a result, OBC leaders often do not perceive LBCs to be qualified for leadership, because the LBCs fail to live up to a cultural standard which OBCs have confused with a spiritual or a biblical standard.[25] As another consequence, LBCs who wish to create a culturally relevant ministry feel powerless to make decisions and lack the financial backing to carry out the decisions they want to make. LBCs often feel that decisions are made to spend money on OBC concerns, while LBC needs go unmet.[26]

Fifth, due to their physical separation from their extended families in their homeland and various cultural factors including discrimination from the host culture, OBCs tend to view the church as an extended hierarchal family (fictive kinship) in which the OBC pastor is the patriarchal leader.[27] Consequently, many OBCs view starting a physically

---

[22] Min, *Korean Protestants*, K.l. 1843–48; Warner, "Introduction," 319–325.

[23] Eng, *FACE*, 85, 119, 146; Jeung, *Faithful Generations*, K.l. 2246–50; Phillips, "Haitian Church," 116–17.

[24] Phillips, "Haitian Church," 103, 117, 120–21, 149–52; Min, *Korean Protestants*, K.l 2992–2994; Rodriguez, *Latino Church*, K.l. 1496–1514; Wong, "Culturally–Sensitive," 76.

[25] Eng, "Overview," 62; Phillips, "Haitian Church," 136; Wong, "Culturally–Sensitive," 82.

[26] Eng, "Programs That Minister Effectively," 146; Fong, *Multi–Asian Ministry*, 184; Jeung, *Faithful Generations*, K.l. 940, 957–60; Min, *Korean Protestants*, K.l. 1878–80; Phillips, "Haitian Church," 121, 139, 145.

[27] Eng, "Effective Model," 114; Justo L. González, *Santa Biblia: The Bible through Hispanic Eyes* (Nashville: Abingdon, 1996), 103–13; Lee, "Silent Exodus," 53–54;

separate LBC ministry and/or investing such a ministry with financial and decision-making power as splitting the family.[28] LBCs frequently want to voice their concerns about unmet needs to OBCs. However, due to cultural differences in what constitutes respectful communication and the fictive kinship understanding of the church as an extended family, even mature LBCs are often perceived by OBCs as being disrespectful to their elders if they attempt to share their concerns about unmet needs.[29] (The fourth and fifth concerns of OBCs likely contribute more than another other factor to OBCs' reticence to transfer financial and decision–making power.)

Sixth, an additional issue contributing to the problem that does not seem to be mentioned by any of the prior sociological studies is that of political context. Many immigrants who come to the United States are coming from totalitarian political systems. These systems generally involve an oppressive authoritarian hierarchy that seeks to maintain its political power through coercion. Ironically, as some immigrants come to the U.S. in order to escape these systems, inevitably due to the human practice of implementing what is familiar and in combination with the previously mentioned factors, immigrants tend to run their church governments in accord with the political systems they left. When immigrant children grow up in the democratic American system that entails free egalitarian rather than totalitarian hierarchal government, then a clash occurs on a practical level between the political ideologies of children involving diffused shared power and those of their immigrant parents involving centralized and exclusive control.

These different cultural concerns between OBCs and LBCs over the retention of financial and decision-making authority by OBCs results in a cycle of tension that, historically and repeatedly, culminates in the LBC exodus from the OBC church. The cycle of tension is that as LBCs begin to voice their concerns, OBCs take measures to hold on to their power. When OBCs hold more tightly to their power, LBCs feel more disenfranchised and may voice their concerns louder, which results in OBCs taking stronger steps to retain their power. The cycle culminates

---

Min, *Korean Protestants*, K.l. 977–79, 1012–13, 1824–27, 1883–84, 227–29; Alex D. Montoya, *Hispanic Ministry in North America* (Grand Rapids: Ministry Resources Library, 1987), 85–86; Phillips, "Haitian Church," 81, 124, 141; Zaki, "Middle Eastern American Church," 44.

[28] Eng, "Overview," 60; Rodriguez, *Latino Church*, K.l. 724–25; Wong, "American–Born Chinese," 46–47.

[29] Eng, "Overview," 71; Phillips, "Haitian Church," 169.

with LBCs leaving the OBC church. The tension is cyclic, because typically all the LBCs will not leave so that the remaining LBCs continue the cycle, and due to continued immigration, new generations of LBCs eventually join the church and repeat the cycle. Furthermore, individuals as well as the whole church may experience the cycle so that the silent exodus occurs one person at a time rather than as a church split. Several solutions have been proposed to resolve this crisis of the immigrant church, but they prove to have a deficient biblical basis and so fail to solve the problem.

Representative OBC/LBC Voices

This section contains excerpts from correspondences that I received in the normal course of ministry along with others that I intentionally solicited from OBC and LBC representatives at various immigrant churches. The authors of these writings gave their permission for their correspondence to be presented anonymously in order to help the immigrant church, and their writings have been edited for content and to ensure anonymity.[30] The purpose of including this correspondence is to illustrate in a concrete and personal way some of the points raised by the impersonal sociological studies of the previous section and to illustrate some of the weaknesses of the three past proposals (bilingual, separate service, and church planting models) described in chapters 4 and 5 in order to aid the reader's understanding and to make the issues come alive. Although the responses do not represent a scientific sample, I believe that they are representative of many OBCs and LBCs in immigrant churches. These responses are not intended to be scientific sociological evidence to support my thesis, but to serve as illustrations to aid understanding. Each group of correspondence is introduced, labeled with some of the issues raised by the authors, and concludes with some questions that may be thought about individually or discussed in a group.

The first two emails were unsolicited correspondences that I received during my years as a pastor of LBC congregations. The first email was written by a college student shortly before leaving the church

---

[30] Some respondents were concerned about backlash against them and only agreed to contribute if they could do so anonymously. Consequently, I asked all of the respondents to contribute anonymously.

and is a composite of three emails sent to me on the issue of leaving the church. The second email was written by a single young adult who had been working in the business world for a few years at the time it was written. Both authors gave permission to use their emails and their statements have been edited for privacy.

LBC Layperson Email #1 (Ethnicity, Joint Service, Meeting Needs): "I'm thinking of leaving [our church] and finding another church. This is why I wasn't at church on Sunday I went to visit a [multiethnic] church. In all honesty, the only change I've seen is changing our name to [a church name that does not include the ethnic identity of the immigrant congregation]. I've been able to not focus on such questions and thoughts for quite some time, feeling that it is my responsibility to stay at church, in some ways thinking that the church needs me more than I need the church. I know that this isn't from God. On Easter Sunday, it finally became too much for me. Sitting in church in the midst of a song in [the OBC language] that had been going on for at least ten minutes and seeing that not even a [LBC] translation was being put up on an overhead, I realized that [the immigrant church] as a whole is not a church that I'm being fed at. When I dread Easter and Christmas because I know that it means joint service, then there is something wrong. Is the concept of a multiracial church something that would divide [the immigrant church]? In light of what I have noticed ... the answer must overwhelmingly be yes. In the midst of all this confusion, only one thing remains clear to me: God's house is supposed to be a house of prayer for all nations, but I feel that [the immigrant church] isn't."

Email #1: Questions for Reflection and Discuss

1. What kind of changes do you think LBCs are looking for based on this e-mail?
2. What is motivating this person to say at their church?
3. Why does this LBC feel that the church is not meeting LBC needs?
4. What reasons does this LBC list as to why activities such as joint service is something they "dread"?
5. What is this LBC's ministry perspective and vision? Is it reaching OBCs and returning to the OBC country of origin as a missionary?

LBC Layperson Email #2 (Transferring Authority to the Next Generation, Leadership and Language, and Cultural Value of Age): "Thanks for giving me the opportunities to serve. I'm really encouraged. I definitely want to plan one of the activities. I will let you know by Sunday which ones. As far as the Church Planning Committee goes, truth is *I hate* meetings. Especially ones where no one speaks the LBC language, and I don't even understand what's going on. Personally I feel that adults have always done things the way they wanted to. Yeah, they say the LBC group is the "future of the church," but they won't really listen to us because we are younger. I don't see myself having an impact on the church."

Email #2: Questions for Reflection and Discussion:

1. Does this LBC want to serve and be involved in leadership?
2. Why does this LBC not want to serve at the "church level" (meetings combined with OBC leaders)?

The next set of correspondence contains excerpts from emails that I intentionally solicited from three LBC leaders at an immigrant church. The three leaders were asked three questions. The following sections lists the question and then the three responses. The LBC leaders replying were in their late twenties to early thirties and were married with young children at the time they responded.

LBC Leaders Question #1: Bilingual Bulletin: Please give your thoughts on having a "bilingual bulletin" every Sunday that has all the church announcements in it (OBC and LBC), with the OBC and LBC languages side by side. Please give your thoughts on whether or not you want or do not want this type of bulletin as well as your thoughts on how this would affect church growth or reaching unbelieving LBCs.

Response #1 to Question #1: "Since we also have Japanese and Koreans at our church, we should also have the bulletin in Japanese and Korean. And if a blind person starts attending our church, we should have the bulletin in Braille. I am strongly opposed to the bilingual bulletin. Practically, there is no need for a bilingual bulletin in the LBC Ministry because over 90% cannot read the OBC language. Also, the bilingual bulletin most likely will hinder growth because the newcomers and visitors to our church will see the bilingual bulletin and assume that the LBC Fellowship still participates in culturally irrelevant activities such as joint services. The new comers and visitors that have come to our church do not want to attend joint services, and a bilingual bulletin will reinforce in their minds that our church is not a church they want to attend. Also, the additional time and resources required to 'coordinate' a bilingual bulletin would strain the LBC Ministry because the people responsible for the LBC bulletin would have to spend more time in obtaining information from the other ministries to put it in the LBC bulletin. If the goal is to communicate important information and announcements from each ministry, that can be done without having a weekly bilingual bulletin, such as email or phone call to the appropriate person who can put that information in each ministry's bulletin."

Response #2 to Question #1: "As for the church bulletin in the OBC language, I do not see the need. What would the point be? Is this regarding the joint services? If so, on those rare times, I think that OBC/LBC language bulletins are helpful. But as for our service, it would be silly. The fact also is that we who type up the programs don't even have the program on our computer. Personally, I don't really care all that much about what the other congregations do (maybe I should), but even if I did, the LBC language is fine with me. Whether it would affect people's attendance? I would hope not. I don't think that it should … to me it seems like a waste of time and money to have such bulletins."

Response #3 to Question #1: "I think this is a waste of time and effort. There's a point where, if there's too much information, people won't read it. This is a bulletin, not a lesson in translation. It's interesting to see at first, but not necessary."

LBC Leaders Question #2: OBC Discipleship: Please give your thoughts on the practicality (personally and culturally speaking, not time availability, etc.) of being discipled by the OBC pastor. In other words, do you feel as an LBC that you would benefit from being discipled by the OBC pastor? If it helps you to think it through, would you want to meet weekly with your OBC pastor for personal one-on-one discipleship?

Response #1 to Question #2: "Weekly one-on-one meetings with our OBC pastor. *Are you crazy*!!! I am opposed to the idea of the OBC pastor pastoring LBC group members. If a pastor's responsibility is to disciple, then the OBC pastor should disciple people in the OBC group and the LBC pastor should disciple people in the LBC group. Having each pastor disciple people in their respective ministries would be more effective because … A. LBC group members are more comfortable with the LBC pastor than the OBC pastor. The LBC pastor is interacting with the LBC group members much more than the [OBC] pastor. Being comfortable, open and honest are important in discipleship, so if these factors are not present, discipleship between the OBC pastor and an LBC member is nearly impossible. B. LBC group members communicate better with the LBC pastor than the OBC pastor. If communication is vital in discipleship, then it is unpractical to have a [OBC] pastor, who cannot speak [the LBC language] well, disciple someone in the LBC group who can only speak [the LBC language]. C. LBC group members have different culture, values and upbringing than the OBC pastor. Therefore, the style and content of discipleship may not suit the LBC group. Why does the OBC pastor want to disciple LBC group members while so many people in the OBC group need to be discipled?"

Response #2 to Question #2: "I would not want discipleship with the OBC pastor. As for the relevancy issue, that too would be a bit strange considering the language barriers."

Response #3 to Question #2: "Just as I told you before, people from another country, unless they're so Americanized, [are] going to walk to the beat of a different drum. The effort and thoughtfulness may be there, but I doubt true communication is being made. I've noticed that whenever I've talked with someone from another country, no matter how often each party says and acts like they understand, there will be times of misunderstanding. Because of the cultural and language background, our perceptions differ."

LBC Leaders Question #3: Parallel Ministry: Please give your thoughts on the necessity of parallel ministry as relating to church growth, the "silent exodus" of LBC people from immigrant churches generally, frustration with joint board meetings and joint services, and any other related issues that you want to briefly address.

Response #1 to Question #3: "I believe that our immigrant church needs to change the existing by-laws to allow the LBC ministry more autonomy and authority to manage its own affairs. Over the years, joint services, joint board meetings, and other joint activities between the OBC and LBC groups have devastated the LBC group. LBC member attendance drops by more than 40% whenever there is a joint service. LBC members refuse to serve as deacons and leaders due to joint board meetings. There are several other issues that frustrate the LBC ministry because the LBC ministry and its members are treated as 'children.' Now the LBC group is not saying we want complete independence or to revolt against the current system. What we are saying is that the current system and traditions are hurting the LBC ministry, and we would like some changes. We are also saying that if the LBC ministry is the future of the immigrant church, then please allow the LBC ministry more autonomy and authority to shape that future. Too many people have left the immigrant church over these issues."

Response #2 to Question #3: "As for the parallel ministry, I think that the church would grow both physically and spiritually at a quicker rate if we had more independence. It would allow us to hire another pastor to pastor the youth with our LBC pastor being free to pastor the adults. This would, of course, help us all (the married with kids, too) by meeting our specific needs and to make our LBC pastor more available for us [the LBC adults]. Right now our LBC pastor is spread pretty thin [pastoring the youth, college and career, and adult/married with children groups]. Whether our church would make a dramatic increase in size, I don't know. I believe we would be able to retain more people and at least create more of a foundation for those at the church, currently."

Response #3 to Question #3: "Whenever I sit in joint meetings/services, I feel like there's no cohesion. There's too much of a break, and my attention drops in the translation. From what I understand, even the translation isn't always accurate. Again, this goes back to my previous comment on cultural and language differences. The meaning and effort are there, but there's going to be a disjunction somewhere. How often do people watch television programs with translations? There probably aren't any, because it wouldn't capture people's attention long enough. Bottom line is what is the ultimate purpose of having joint services/meetings? I don't see any unity being formed, unless it's unity in vicinity."

Questions for Reflection and Discussion on the Three LBC Leader's Questions and Answers:

1. What insight do these comments on a bilingual bulletin give you into LBC's thinking about joint events generally?
2. If LBC lay people do not want to be discipled by the OBC pastor, then why do we expect LBC pastors to be discipled in this way?
3. LBC pastors and laypeople are often criticized as trying to "get more power" and being divisive for promoting parallel ministry rather than being recognized as genuinely seeking the needs

and desires of their congregations. Given the comments above, does this criticism seem to be true?

The following email was solicited from an LBC pastor regarding specific questions:

LBC Pastor Question: #1: What are some frustrations that you had working with the immigrant pastor and leadership?

Response to Question #1: "My relationships with our OBC pastors were actually very good.31 But here are the challenges we had: (1) Communication: The immigrant pastor did not have a mastery of English, so he could not always express himself when we met. Likewise, I could not speak the OBC language, so we had limitations that would occasionally hinder our communication. (2) Control: I worked with two OBC pastors, both were very trusting and they granted me a tremendous amount of autonomy. But the OBC board was not always as willing to impart control of the LBC ministry to the LBC leadership.32 This led to conflict and frustration. When the OBC leadership was willing to empower and compromise, the LBC ministry flourished. When the OBC leadership insisted on controlling the ministry, the LBC ministry was stifled and divided. At two points more than half our LBC congregation members left our LBC congregation because the OBC leadership would not listen to their appeals."

LBC Pastor Question #2: If you could give immigrant pastors frank and direct advice on how to work well with the LBC pastor and LBC leaders, what would you tell them?

Response to Question #2: "(1) Hire well: Do not choose your LBC pastor based on his degrees or on your desperate need for help. Make sure that you find someone who you can trust. Find a pastor who is called to minister in the context of an immigrant church and who understands

---

[31] In my experience, this LBC pastor had a better relationship with his OBC pastors than most LBC pastors typically do. I believe it is in part due to his exceptionally virtuous Christian character.

[32] Regarding this comment, it is important to remember that in some churches the (OBC) pastor runs the church, while in other churches the board retains the ruling power and the pastor merely preaches, teaches, and counsels, etc. Ideally, there is an accountability relationship between the board and pastor, but this rarely occurs in actual practice.

OBC culture. (2) Empower your LBC pastor and LBC leaders. The LBC ministry functions best when it operates as a church within the church—not as a department of the church. Let the LBC leadership lead the ministry, because they know best what it takes to reach other English-speaking LBCs. Use Acts 6 as your model for this. (3) Expand your view of the Kingdom of God: Many of the conflicts that arise in immigrant churches come out of cultural expectations. God's Kingdom supersedes all cultures. Let the Holy Spirit lead each generation and subculture of the church in ways that are uniquely suited to serve and reach that generation. Don't insist that others follow your deeply held cultural practices."

Questions for Reflection and Discussion on the LBC Pastoral Response:

1. Can OBC pastors effectively manage LBC pastors with whom they cannot communicate due to a language barrier and cultural differences? How would the elimination of a reporting relationship through the establishment of co-pastors impact the tension between the OBC and LBC pastor?
2. What single factor helped the LBC congregation to grow? Why was this factor helpful?
3. Can you think of three to five ministry practices, social customs, or theological beliefs that LBCs and OBCs respectively hold that are based more on culture than Scripture?

The following responses were solicited from an OBC pastor during a phone interview. His responses have been edited and summarized based on a transcript of the phone call and synthesized with a written outline he provided by email. He was asked to respond to a series of questions.

OBC Pastor Question #1: What are some frustrations that you have had working with English pastors and/or leadership?

Response to Question #1: "I am going to share not only my personal frustrations, but also some of the observations of other OBC pastors. I would like to share three frustrations regarding: (1) family baggage, (2) differences in the way of doing ministry, and (3) cultural reaction."

"*Family Baggage*: First, the LBC pastor's family baggage impacts their ministry in ways that are frustrating for OBC pastors. Currently in many immigrant churches, an LBC is the pastor over the LBC congregation. These LBCs are the second generation who grew up in the immigrant church. Many of them have had generational, cultural, and language struggles with their parents. Many times, the OBC parents communicate (their love) differently or simply do not communicate. All of this creates a gap between the first and second generations. So for many, if not most, LBCs, they have not had a positive experience with their parents and the general family atmosphere is quite tense. Consequently, many LBC pastors carry this tension, this baggage, from their family of origin into the church family. They view themselves and the English congregation as victims, they view the board and their supervisor as unreasonable parents, and they view themselves as second class citizens. I and other OBC pastors have heard personally from LBC pastors that their mission is, like Moses, to liberate the LBC people to flee from the bondage of the OBC church. Therefore, in the church, there is an inherent tension that has nothing to do with the actual behavior, but rather is a part of a hidden psychological inclination or baggage on the part of the LBCs."

"*Differences in the Way of Doing Ministry*: Second, differences in the way LBCs want to do ministry are frustrating to OBCs. LBCs do not agree with the way the OBCs do things, because they think that it is my parent's way of doing things—it is the OBC way of doing things. Sometimes they will use this cultural difference to cover up their unwillingness to perform the job properly. For example, OBCs still practice Billy Graham style crusade or mass evangelism, hold a traditional Sunday school, and have midweek prayer meeting at the church. Instead, LBCs want to do friendship or relational evangelism, have fellowship during the Sunday school time, and hold prayer meetings in their homes rather than at church. This is not totally wrong, however, while LBCs oppose everything the OBC church is doing, frequently, LBCs have not yet built an alternate way of doing these things. For example, if discipleship and Christian education are not practiced in Sunday school, where will they occur? The way of doing ministry does need to be renewed from time to time, but if traditional programs are done well, then they may still be effective."

"*Cultural Reaction*: Third, how the LBCs reaction to American or perhaps OBC culture influences their perspective and performance of ministry is frustrating to OBC pastors. The American culture is dominated by an air of professionalism. Professionalism is not necessarily a bad thing. However, many LBC pastors love the Lord, but follow the American culture in viewing themselves as a professional. Consequently, they view their ministry more as a career than a calling from God. For example, when we interview for a new LBC staff position, candidates frequently demonstrate that they are too focused on the position as a career by asking about days off, vacation, salary level, and benefits. They treat it as a professional position. On the other hand, their professionalism may be a reaction to OBC culture, which is very performance oriented. For example, there is a lot of pressure on LBCs growing up to perform academically in order to secure a future career. Therefore, when LBCs enter ministry, they may express this performance orientation as professionalism. However, some LBC pastors react to the performance orientation of OBC culture on the other end of the spectrum by being too laid back and failing to perform their job well."

"In sharing all these things, I am speaking from the perspective of a typical OBC pastor, so my observations may not be totally correct. I could be wrong, but these are the things I have observed from my perspective. I have my own personal standards and understanding of ministry too, which I hope are in alignment with biblical values and a biblical perspective. My view is not perfect, but this is how I see things, and these are some of the frustrations I have experienced working with LBCs and LBC pastors."

OBC Pastor Question #2: If you could give LBC pastors frank and direct advice on how to work well with the OBC pastor and church board, what would you tell them?

Response to Question #2: "There are three pieces of advice I would like to pass on to LBC pastors to encourage them to work effectively in an immigrant church. This advice involves the LBC pastor's (1) self-identity, (2) ministry identity as a missionary-pastor, and (3) proactive communication. *"Self-Identity*: First, the LBC pastor needs to have a healthy mindset about his own identity. Some LBC pastors have a conflict over their self-identity since they do not fit into the mainstream culture or into the OBC culture. When this is the case, the LBC pastor tends to project this identity crisis onto both the people to whom they minister and onto those to whom they report, and this projection causes tension in the church. The LBC pastor should look to Moses as an example in order to find peace about their self-identity. Moses was a Jew who was born in Egypt, and he was rejected by both the Jews and Egyptians. However, God had a special plan for Moses' unique identity in the history of salvation. Similarly, LBCs have a unique identity and a special plan in God's Kingdom and in their role in ministering in the OBC church. The successful LBC pastor will have a settled self-identity because they recognize and accept the special role of their unique cultural identity in God's Kingdom."

"Ministry Identity: Second, the LBC pastor has a choice whether to serve in an immigrant church or in a church of the mainstream culture. Since the immigrant church is a foreign mission field in the country of residence, then the successful LBC pastor will view their professional identity as a missionary-pastor. As in cross-cultural missions, due to the cultural and language differences, serving in an immigrant church requires perhaps more time, energy, tolerance, and patience, than a church in the mainstream culture. As a missionary-pastor, the successful LBC pastor will: (1) seek to understand all the cultures in the church, (2) seek the good of the church rather than the special needs of his own congregation, (3) seek not to conform the OBC church to the mainstream culture, and (4) seek to go the extra mile. Therefore, LBC pastors should count the cost before serving in an immigrant church and serve elsewhere, in either an LBC or mainstream church, if they are not willing to make the necessary sacrifices involved in a missionary ministry."

"Communication: Third, depending on their culture, the OBC senior pastor and board may tend not to be very communicative and may not be very direct. They may hide initial anger, resentment, and displeasure that may finally explode on a later occasion. Therefore, the LBC pastor should be more proactive in communicating with the OBC pastor and the board and should never "bypass the boss" to accomplish ministry goals."

OBC Pastor Question #3: Are there any general thoughts about the challenges of being an immigrant pastor in an immigrant church in America with an English-speaking/LBC congregation that you would want either the immigrant or English-speaking/LBC ministries to understand?

Response to Question #3: "I would like to offer several suggestions to both OBC and LBC pastors. First, I would like to suggest that the OBC pastor needs to spend more time trying to understand LBCs in general, but particularly their frustrations, heart-language/culture, and values. Some OBCs are educated abroad, but they never spend enough time to understand the heart-language/culture of the young people, and consequently, they miss the deeper meaning of their words and fail to understand. This effort to understand may even involve listening to the music and watching the movies in which LBCs are interested, rather than merely watching OBC media from home or produced locally."

"I would also like to suggest that both the OBC and LBC pastors should strive to put more emphasis on unity rather than uniformity. Additionally, both the OBC and LBC pastors should understand the difference between the shape of the church and the essence of the church. The shape of the church is the way of doing ministry. It includes such things as whether or not the church has Sunday school, has midweek prayer meetings, recites the Lord's prayer, memorizes the Apostle's Creed in service, etc. The essence of the church is what the church really is or what are the basic elements that make a church, a church. The essence includes such things as doctrine, theological conviction, and moral and ethical application of doctrine. For example, the essence of water is H_2O, transparent, tasteless, and odorless. The shape of water is merely the container in which it is placed, say a bottle or a bowl. The bottle or bowl shape does not make the water, water, but rather its chemical composition and properties determine its essence. There should be agreement upon the essence of the church, but in the shape of the church, there should be some flexibility in the way of doing things. Give each other space to take your own shape or do things your own way and do not criticize each other."

"Finally, both OBCs and LBCs should follow Romans 15:1-7 and 1 Corinthians 10:23-11:1 in giving respect to the weaker brother. For example, the OBCs should show respect to the LBCs even though they may be smaller in size and weaker in offering. If the LBCs are larger and stronger, then they should show respect to the OBCs."

Questions for Reflection and Discussion on the OBC Pastoral Response:

1. What is the primary biblical image of the church or way that the OBC pastor thinks of the nature of the church in his response to the first question?
2. Do joint services promote uniformity or unity? Why? What are some ways of promoting unity rather than uniformity in multilingual, multigenerational, and multi-congregational, immigrant churches?
3. What is the difference between the shape and essence of the church? Do you agree that such a difference exists? What are some ways that the immigrant church can foster unity of essence, while promoting diversity of shape?

The following email was solicited from an OBC retired couple whose children are grown and have their own kids. This couple was told that one of the problems the immigrant church faces is that the English/LBC ministry is usually ineffective in meeting the needs of immigrant children because of cultural and language expectations in the church. Consequently, many immigrant children either leave the immigrant church or fall away from the faith because the church did not effectively minister to them and/or preach to them the Gospel. They were also told that many immigrant parents like them are heartbroken because, when their children grew up, they left the church and/or fell away from the faith. Since this is a very painful topic for parents to share with others, they usually do not warn younger immigrants so that they can make changes in the church to help avoid this problem.

The retired couple was asked to share the story of one of their children who left the church and fell away from the faith and what role they thought the church played in the process. Although they speak fluent English, due to the sensitive and painful nature of the issue, they shared their response with one of their children who has stayed in the church, and this child responded by email with the following response that has been edited.

OBC Parents Response: "We do not really know for sure what happened to our child, but this is our perspective on their spiritual journey. Our church had a cultural and language barrier and [did not have] many people of the same age and background for our child to be friends with. Also, the church kept having many changes, with no steady pastor and no steady youth leader to guide the LBC congregation. Also, the OBC service had problems with people arguing amongst themselves. This caused our child to be disappointed with the people at church. It seemed like they did not really love one another."

"Our child decided to leave. After moving away from home, our child attended a church of the mainstream culture. Our child liked this church because it was multicultural and was subsequently baptized at that church. After moving to another state, our child could not find a similar kind of church to attend. Once, a co-worker invited our child to a multicultural OBC church nearby. After a onetime visit, our child stopped going to church."

"When our child and spouse come to visit, they will pray before eating and will go to an LBC church. We have asked our child twice to re-dedicate their life to Jesus Christ. We are seeing changes in our child's life, and we hope and pray that it continues with the help of Christ."

Questions for Reflection and Discussion on the LBC Pastoral Response:

1. Of the factors the parents felt contributed to their child leaving the immigrant church, which are factors unique to the OBC church, and which might be common to any church?
2. Due to culture and the strong emotions involved, the OBC parents did not share much of their feelings in their factual response. How do you think they felt as their child passed through the different stages of their spiritual journey described in the story?

Having presented the evidence from sociological studies and the responses of some OBC and LBC leaders and laypeople, it is hoped that the reader has a good grasp of the crisis that the immigrant church faces. It is likely that various cultures will identify more with some of the OBC and LBC concerns expressed and less with others. However, the representative list of concerns presented earlier in this chapter and the various OBC/LBC voices may help people of any culture to begin to identify any concerns particular to their own culture. Regardless of specific cultural concerns or challenges, the main ecclesiastical crisis that the immigrant church faces is a complex of cultural and linguistic factors that create a reticence on the part of immigrants to transfer financial and decision-making authority to succeeding generations. This results in a culturally irrelevant ministry to those generations, an exodus of believers from the church, a spiritually immature remnant, and an inability to reach the lost.

Parallel ministry, based on Acts 6:1-7, is the biblical solution to the crisis in the immigrant church. The next two chapters will present the current proposal of parallel ministry through a detailed exegesis of Acts 6:1-7 and will highlight the ways parallel ministry solves the crisis of the immigrant church. Chapters 4 and 5 will then present the alternative solutions historically proposed and typically practiced to address the crisis and expose how they are theoretically deficient and practically fail to meet the needs of both OBCs and LBCs.

CHAPTER 2. Current Proposal: Exegesis of Acts 6:1-7

Although parallel processing had been used for decades, when the Intel Corporation first released its dual-core processor for commercial use in 2006, the term "parallel processing" became fixed in the public consciousness.[1] Parallel computing is "a form of computation in which many calculations are carried out simultaneously, operating on the principle that large problems can often be divided into smaller ones, which are then solved concurrently" or in parallel.[2] One method of "parallel" computing is not only to solve the smaller parts of a larger problem separately and simultaneously, but also to combine the results into a single solution.[3] For example, suppose one wanted to calculate the sum of the

---

[1] Robert J. Benson, Pieter M. Ribbers, and Ronald B. Blitstein, *Trust and Partnership: Strategic IT Management for Turbulent Times*, Wiley CIO Series (Hoboken, NJ: Wiley, 2014), 118; N. B. Venkateswarlu, *Essential Computer and IT Fundamentals for Engineering and Science Students* (Ram Nagar, New Delhi: S. Chand, 2012), 51.

[2] Mehdi Khosrow-Pour, ed. *Dictionary of Information Science and Technology*, 2nd ed., vol. 1 (Hershey, PA: Information Science Reference, 2013), s.v. "Parallel Computing." See also: D. V. Lukyanenko and A. G. Yagola, "Using Parallel Computing for Solving Multidimensional Ill-Posed Problems," in *Computational Methods for Applied Inverse Problems*, ed. Yanfei Wang, Anatoly G. Yagola, and Yang. Changchun, vol. 56 of Inverse and Ill-Posed Problems Series (Boston: Higher Education, 2012), 51.

[3] Vladimir Janjaic, Christopher Brown, and Kevin Hammond, "Lapedo: Hybrid Skeletons for Programming Heterogeneous Multicore Machines in Erlang" in *Parallel Computing: On the Road to Exascale*, ed. Gerhard R. Joubert et al. (Washington, D.C.: IOS, 2016), 189.

equation 1 + 2 + 3 + 4. Hypothetically, a dual-core processor might break the problem up into 1 + 2 = 3 and 3 + 4 = 7 in order to solve the equation. After achieving the results 3 and 7, they would be combined into the single solution of 10.

As two types of "parallel" concepts, parallel processing and parallel ministry have some similarities. As parallel processing developed into a solution to a number of problems in computing—cost effectiveness, performance (computing speed, volume, and complexity), and heat generation—likewise, in Acts 6:1-7, what is now called parallel ministry was developed as a biblical solution to a situation that is similar to the contemporary crisis of the immigrant church between OBCs and LBCs.[4] Just as parallel processing involves two aspects of computers, the software (algorithms) and the hardware (architecture), so parallel ministry has two aspects, the spiritual-relational and the ecclesiastical.[5] Remember that the spiritual-relational aspect includes such things as changed attitudes, and the ecclesial aspect, that is the focus of this book, involves how the church should be structured. As the hardware and software are in an interdependent relationship in parallel processing so that both are required to work together for a computer to run properly, so too in parallel ministry both the spiritual-relational and ecclesiastical aspects are necessary for the solution to work.[6]

Similar to parallel processing's division of tasks into the dual-cores of one computer in the example of calculating the sum of the equation 1 + 2 + 3 + 4, parallel ministry in Acts 6:1-7 solves the immigrant church crisis by handling the different concerns of OBCs and LBCs in one church but simultaneously through separate, interdependent, and parallel ecclesiastical elements. These elements include, but are not necessarily limited to, two services, two offerings, two budgets, two boards, two visions, and two co-pastors respectively for OBCs and LBCs. Just as in parallel processing, the results of each parallel ecclesiastical element of OBCs and LBCs respectively are combined to meet the needs and reach the lost of the whole immigrant church and the larger Kingdom of God.

---

[4] Ibid., 1, 8.

[5] Behrooz Parhami, *Introduction to Parallel Processing: Algorithms and Architectures*, Plenum Series in Computer Science (New York: Kluwer, 2002), 1.

[6] Jean-Michel Bergé, Oz Levia, and Jacques Rouillard, eds., *Hardware/Software Co-Design and Co-Verification*, Current Issues in Electronic Modeling, vol. 8 (Boston: Kluwer, 1997), 2.

The similarities between parallel processing and parallel ministry also help to distinguish parallel ministry from and to demonstrate the deficiencies of the alternative solutions to the crisis of the immigrant church discussed in chapters 4 and 5. These alternatives to parallel ministry include bilingual worship, separate worship services, and church planting. Bilingual worship involves using some type of translation between the OBC and LBC languages, typically only in a worship service. Separate services involve different worship services for OBCs and LBCs that meet at different times and/or locations. Church planting seeks to plant LBC churches that are independent from OBC churches. Returning to the analogy, although the terms "parallel processing" and "concurrent processing" are often used synonymously in computer literature, the expressions are distinct and should not be confused.[7] In order to contrast it with concurrent processing, parallel processing may be defined as breaking a single task down into sub-tasks on two or more central processing units (CPUs).[8] Concurrent processing may be understood as multitasking unrelated tasks by time-sharing on a single-core or CPU.[9]

Similarly, to the difference between parallel and concurrent processing, in parallel ministry sociology and theology are different fields of study and should not be confused. One difference between parallel ministry and other solutions—bilingual ministry, separate services, and church planting—is how sociology and theology are used. Parallel ministry uses sociology to define the crisis of the immigrant church, but uses theology to solve the problem, while the other solutions confuse sociology and theology by using sociology to not only define the problem, but as part of the solution. Such confusion in these other solutions compromises the sufficiency and authority of Scripture. Just as parallel processing is a good comparison or a valid analogy to parallel ministry, so the situation in Acts 6:1-7 that parallel ministry uses as an ecclesiological solution is similar to or a valid analogy to the contemporary crisis in the immigrant church. In the other solutions to the crisis—bilingual ministry,

---

[7] Clay Breshears, The Art of Concurrency: A Thread Monkey's Guide to Writing Parallel Applications (Beijing: O'Reilly, 2009), 3.

[8] Ibid., 3.

[9] Ibid., 3.

separate services, and church planting—biblical passages are used that are invalid analogies or poor comparisons to the crisis in the immigrant church. Whereas parallel ministry metaphorically uses addition as a solution in the parallel processing analogy, the other solutions to the crisis use deficient solutions symbolically involving division, multiplication, and subtraction.

In this chapter, the tool of sociology used to define the problem in chapter 1 is set aside in order to explain in detail how the parallel ministry model is derived from Acts 6:1-7 and how it solves the crisis of the immigrant church. Some attention is also given to compare parallel ministry to the alternate solutions in order to demonstrate their deficiency. A detailed exegesis of Acts 6:1-7 demonstrates that the ecclesiastical parallel ministry structure exists when favorable spiritual-relational conditions occur in such a way that OBCs transfer financial and decision-making authority to LBCs so that they may create a culturally relevant interdependent ministry that allows for the needs of both groups to be met. In this interpretation of Acts 6:1-7, the passage explicitly and implicitly states that the parallel ministry ecclesiastical structure consists not only of separate and culturally relevant OBC and LBC worship services, but also co-pastors and different offerings, budgets, boards, and visions that are part of a single interdependent church. The various elements that make up the structure are "parallel" because while OBCs and LBCs each have their separate respective ecclesiastical components, those components are interdependent rather than independent or dependent upon each other.

Acts 6:1-7 is the definitive passage for dealing with the crisis of the immigrant church, because it resolves a cultural conflict similar to the one between contemporary OBCs and LBCs (valid analogy). It also provides explicit principles and implied details that are used to construct the parallel ministry ecclesiological model and, at the same time, exclude the bilingual, separate service, and church planting models.

In the familiar passage of Acts 6:1-7, the account is given of a cultural dispute within the early church whereby the Hellenistic Jewish Christians charged the Hebraic Jewish Christians with not meeting the needs of Hellenist widows in the distribution of daily support. The dispute was resolved by the whole church's acceptance of the apostles' proposal to delegate the task of distributing support to leaders that the community selected and the apostles commissioned. Seven Hellenistic leaders, including Stephen and Philip, were assigned the task of meeting the widows' needs. As a result, the church continued to grow by reaching unbelievers. The passage indicates that cultural conflicts between groups similar to OBCs and LBCs are resolved by transferring financial and decision-making power to the LBCs so that they may have a culturally relevant ministry that meets their needs and has the capacity to reach the lost.

The exegesis of Acts 6:1-7 will proceed in two parts. First, six points are drawn from the text that are explicitly present in the meaning of Acts 6:1-7. These points form the basic outline or definition of parallel ministry. Second, five additional points are drawn from the text, which are implications of the meaning and are supplemental to the basic definition of parallel ministry.

The Basic Outline of Parallel Ministry

The following six points indicate how the basic outline of parallel ministry is derived from the textual details of the narrative in Acts 6:1-7.

(1) *Valid Analogy*: It is important to establish that Acts 6:1-7 presents a "valid analogy" or an example that can be accurately compared to the cultural situation of OBCs and LBCs in the contemporary immigrant church. In Acts 6:1, there is a significant amount of scholarly debate over how the terms "Ἑβραίους" [Hebraic Jews] and "Ἑλληνιστῶν" [Hellenistic Jews] should be translated or who their identities are. The discussion questions whether these terms refer to merely linguistic, merely cultural, or to both cultural and linguistic attributes of the two groups or whether they refer to some sort of doctrinal rift over differences in interpretation of the Mosaic Law.

In the current debate, there seems to be a scholarly consensus that Acts 6:1 does not refer to doctrinal differences, but rather indicates that there were two groups of the same ethnicity that were differentiated by cultural-linguistic factors.[10] On this reading, the term "Ἑβραίους" refers

---

[10] Darrell L. Bock, *Acts*, BECNT (Grand Rapids: Baker Academic, 2007), in *Logos Library System* [CD–ROM], 258; Craig S. Keener, *Acts: An Exegetical Commentary*, Kindle ed., vol. 2 (Grand Rapids: Baker Academic, 2013), K.l. 8537–41, 8574, 8579–80, 8628, 8630–32, 8657–58, 8661–62; Ricahrd N. Longenecker, *The Acts of the Apostles*, ed. Frank E. Gaebelein and J. D. Douglas, in vol. 9 of *EBC* (Grand Rapids: Zondervan, Regency Reference Library, 1981), in *QuickVerse* [CD–ROM], (Grand Rapids, MI: The Zondervan Corporation, 1976), 329, 332; Mikeal C. Parsons, *Acts*, PCNT (Grand Rapids: Baker Academic, 2008), in *Logos Library System* [CD-ROM],

to "Hebraic Jews" who grew up in Palestine, spoke Aramaic as their first language, and were less Hellenized (assimilated to Greek culture). Likewise, the term "Ἑλληνιστῶν" refers to "Hellenistic Jews" who spoke Greek as their first language, were more Hellenized, and were part of the diaspora (Jews scattered outside Palestine/Jerusalem) who had returned to live in Jerusalem.

Significantly, Keener argues that the "the Hellenists to whom Luke refers are probably the Diaspora immigrants...like various immigrant congregations today, included second-generation members who had grown up in Jerusalem."[11] In Acts 6:1, both the "Ἑβραίους" and "Ἑλληνιστῶν" are grouped among the disciples whose numbers were increasing and had widows who were receiving daily support from the church, so in this context, both terms refer to "Jewish Christians." As Polhill notes, in Acts 6:1, the "Ἑλληνιστῶν" consisted "exclusively of Jews," as Nicolas the convert or "proselyte" is an "exception" due to the fact that the Gentile mission had not begun yet.[12]

The Jerusalem church was not a multiethnic church as some may claim, but rather was an ethnically Jewish church with Aramaic and Greek speaking Jews at different levels of assimilation to the Greco–Roman culture. Consequently, the "Ἑβραίους" [Hebraic Jews] are analogous to contemporary OBCs and "Ἑλληνιστῶν" [Hellenistic Jews] are comparable to contemporary LBCs. Furthermore, the term "γογγυσμὸς" [complaint] (Acts 6:1), indicates that the two cultural-linguistic groups were having a conflict. Therefore, the situation in Acts 6:1-7 of two cultural-linguistic groups of the same ethnicity (Hebraic and Hellenistic *Jews*) having a dispute is similar to or a valid analogy to the contemporary situation of a conflict between two cultural-linguistic groups of the same ethnicity, namely OBCs (similar to Hebraic Jews) and their LBC children (similar to Hellenistic Jews) in contemporary churches.

One problem with the alternative solutions to the crisis of the immigrant church is that they do not use valid analogies. As the foregoing analysis demonstrates, the situation in Acts 6:1-7 used to construct the

---

82; John B. Polhill, *Acts*, NAC, vol. 26 (Nashville: Broadman & Holman, 1995), in *Logos Library System* [CD–ROM], 178–79; Ben Witherington, III, *The Acts of the Apostles: A Socio–Rhetorical Commentary* (Grand Rapids: W. B. Eerdmans, 1998), in *Logos Library System* [CD–ROM], 240–42, 250.

[11] Craig S. Keener, *Acts 3:1–14:28*, K.l. 2:8657–58.

[12] Polhill, *Acts*, 178.

parallel ministry model is analogous to the contemporary crisis of the immigrant church. The next point further strengthens the validity of the analogy.

(2) *Unmet Needs*: The nature of the conflict between the Hebraic Jewish Christians and the Hellenistic Jewish Christians is analogous to that between OBCs and LBCs in that the needs of one group were not being met by the other group. In Acts 6:1, it was the Hellenists (LBCs) who were complaining about the Hebraists (OBCs). The same verse explicitly defines the nature of the complaint as being that the Hellenists' "widows were being neglected in the daily distribution." The phrase "τῇ διακονίᾳ τῇ καθημερινῇ" [lit. daily ministry] has been variously understood as referring to money, food, and even clothes, but whatever the details, it refers the basic survival needs of those being helped.[13] Furthermore, in Acts 6:3 the statement of the problem resolution explicitly refers to putting seven men in charge of "τῆς χρείας ταύτης," which is not literally a "responsibility" (NIV) or a "task" (NAS), but rather "this need" (BDAG; Young's Literal Translation), highlighting that the problem resolved in the passage was one of unmet needs.[14]

In Acts 6:1, the term "παρεθεωροῦντο" [overlooked or neglected] demonstrates that the needs of the Hellenists were not met by the Hebraists. Most scholars, despite the fact that they acknowledge that strong Hebraic and Hellenistic tensions existed, incredibly deny discrimination was an issue. Their denial is based in large part on the fact that the disciples were the ones in charge of the distribution (Acts 4:34-37, 5:2), and these scholars point instead to the widows being accidently "overlooked" due to the church's rapid growth (Acts 6:1).[15] The possibility has even been entertained that the term "γογγυσμὸς"

---

[13] Bock, Acts, 257; Keener, *Acts 3:1–14:28*, K.l. 2:8758–62; Polhill, *Acts*, 180.

[14] Arndt, BDAG, s.v. "χρεία."

[15] Bock, *Acts*, 258; I. Howard Marshall, *The Acts of the Apostles: An Introduction and Commentary*, Reprint ed., TNTC, vol. 5 (Grand Rapids: William B. Eerdmans, 1989), 125; David G. Peterson, *The Acts of the Apostles*, PNTC (Grand Rapids: W.B. Eerdmans, 2009), in *Logos Library System* [CD–ROM], 231; Polhill, *Acts*, 179–80; Witherington, *Acts*, 249; Stanley D. Toussaint, "Acts," in *BKC*, ed. John F. Walvoord and Roy B. Zuck (Wheaton, IL: Victor Books, 1985), in *Logos Library System* [CD–ROM], 2:367.

[complaint] is used by Luke to shift blame from the Hebraists to the Hellenists by painting the Hellenists in a bad light because of the pejorative use of the term elsewhere in Scripture (Luke 5:30, 15:2, 19:7; LXX: Ex. 16:7–9, 12, 17:3; Num. 11:1 ff.; 14:27, 29, 16:41, 17:5, 10; Ps. 106:25).[16]

However, several factors suggest that those scholars are correct who find discrimination as at least part of the problem in the passage.[17] One factor is that Luke mentions the growth (Acts 6:1), not as the cause of the conflict, but rather as a mitigating factor to soften the dispute. Such a softening intent is indicated by the fact that, while Luke has explicitly identified the apostles as the one's responsible for the distribution (Acts 4:34-37; 5:2) in Acts 6:1, the complaint is lodged against the Hebraists rather than the apostles. At the same time, it was the apostles who were the ones who acknowledged responsibility for the complaint by resolving it (Acts 6:2).[18]

Another factor is that the lexical evidence allows for the term "παρεθεωροῦντο" to mean "neglect" (BDAG) or even "*neglect*, as the result of making an unfavorable comparison," which implies intent to discriminate (ALGNT).[19] Decisively, Luke's explicit mention of the two cultural groups ("Ἑβραίους" [Hebraic Jews] and "Ἑλληνιστῶν" [Hellenistic Jews] in Acts 6:1) highlights their well-known historical cultural conflicts and colors the context as having to do with cultural

---

[16] Keener, *Acts 3:1–14:28*, K.l. 2:8704–25. Among others, Keener appeals to Bonsirven for support: Joseph Bonsirven, *Palestinian Judaism in the Time of Jesus Christ* (New York: Holt, Rinehart & Winston, 1964), 58.

[17] F. F. Bruce, *The Book of Acts*, Revised ed., NICNT (Grand Rapids: William B. Eerdmans, 1988), 120; Keener, *Acts 3:1–14:28*, K.l. 2:8519–20, 8817–19; Darin Hawkins Land, *The Diffusion of Ecclesiastical Authority: Sociological Dimensions of Leadership in the Book of Acts*, Princeton Theological Monograph Series, vol. 90, Kindel ed. (Eugene, OR: Pickwick, 2008), K.l. 3659; Longenecker, *Acts*, 330.

[18] For a similar judgment see: Keener, *Acts 3:1–14:28*, K.l. 2:8687 ff.; Land, *Diffusion of Ecclesiastical Authority*, K.l. 3641–43, 3648–50; Longenecker, *Acts*, 330.

[19] Emphasis original. Arndt, BDAG, s.v. "παραθεωρέω;" Alfred Edersheim, *The Life and Times of Jesus the Messiah*, 8th, Revised ed. (New York: Longmans, Green, and Co., 1962), 1:7–9; Timothy Friberg, Barbara Friberg, and Neva F. Miller, ed. *Analytical Lexicon of the Greek New Testament*, Baker's Greek New Testament Library (Grand Rapids: Baker Books, 2000), in *Logos Library System* [CD–ROM], s.v. "παραθεωρέω."

issues such as discrimination.[20] Therefore, in Acts 6:1 the nature of the conflict is that the Hellenistic Jews were complaining that the Hebraic Jews were not meeting their needs, possibly due to cultural discrimination.

Analogously in the contemporary immigrant church, the LBCs are complaining that the OBCs are not meeting their needs. Similar to the Hebraic Jews withholding support for daily needs from the Hellenistic Jews because of cultural discrimination, LBC needs go unmet due to cultural discrimination when OBCs disqualify LBCs from leadership because LBCs fail to meet OBC cultural standards of spiritual maturity as discussed in chapter 1. LBCs spiritual needs are also unmet when OBCs attempt to preserve their language and culture through the church by using ecclesiastical models such as bilingual ministry for the purpose of accomplishing this goal, but with the actual result of creating culturally irrelevant ministries that alienate LBCs from the church. The joint services of the separate service model result in the same alienation of LBCs. Likewise, the church planting model meets the needs of some LBCs by providing them a culturally relevant ministry, but removes some LBCs from the immigrant church so that the OBC need to have their remaining children and new immigrant children cared for goes unmet. As in Acts 6:1, when OBCs act to meet LBCs needs through the institution of parallel ministry, only then are the needs of both groups most fully met.

Therefore, both the existence of two cultural groups of the same ethnicity and the fact that they are in conflict over unmet needs establish a valid analogy between the situation in Acts 6:1-7 and the contemporary crisis of the immigrant church. The following points demonstrate that the use of Acts 6:1-7 by the parallel ministry model establishes a valid analogy to the contemporary crisis, not only through the similarity of the situations, but also because in the passage an ecclesiological solution is offered to the problem presented. The alternative solutions to parallel ministry use invalid analogies, not only because the situation of the biblical passages they apply to the contemporary crisis of the immigrant church is not similar, but also because these other deficient solutions use spiritual-relational passages rather than ecclesiological ones to solve the crisis.

---

[20] The discrimination in the passage is cultural and not racial, because both the Hebraists and Hellenists were Jews.

(3) *Transfer of Financial Authority*: In Acts 6:2, the apostles (OBCs) resolved the conflict by transferring financial authority from themselves (Acts 4:34-37, 5:2), the Hebraists (Acts 6:1-2), to the Hellenistic Jews (LBCs, Acts 6:5). In Acts 6:2, there are at least three positions regarding the term "τραπέζαις" [tables]:

a. It refers to the "money lender's bench" or a "bank" (cp. Luke 19:23; see also: Matt. 21:12; Mark 11:15; John 2:15; BDAG, Bruce, Parsons, Toussaint).
b. b. The term does not refer to "banks," but the ministry in the passage still involved money (Keener, Peterson).
c. c. And neither "banks" nor finances are in view in the passage (Longenecker).[21]

The interpretation of the term "τραπέζαις" [tables] (Acts 6:2), depends in part on the type of alms giving that is described by the phrase "τῇ διακονίᾳ τῇ καθημερινῇ" [daily ministry/distribution] (Acts 6:1).[22] To interpret the type of charity described by the phrase "τῇ διακονίᾳ τῇ καθημερινῇ" (Acts 6:2), appeal is made to the Talmud and b. B. Bat. Of particular importance is 8B, for it describes Jewish charity practices thought to be in force at the time.

> C. Food for the soup kitchen is collected by three and passed out by three, since it is passed out as soon as it is collected. Food is passed out every day, money from the charity fund on Fridays. D. The soup kitchen is for everybody, the charity fund is limited to the poor of the town.[23]

In b. B. Bat. 8B, there are two types of charities: "the soup kitchen" [תַּמְחוּי/*tamḥūy*] and "the charity fund" [(קוּפָּה/*quppāh*)].[24] The "soup kitchen" involved the daily distribution of food and was for

[21] Arndt, BDAG, s.v. "τράπεζα"; Bruce, *Acts*, 122; Keener, *Acts 3:1–14:28*, K.l. 2:4887–89, 8865, 8949–52; Longenecker, *Acts*, 332; Parsons, *Acts*, 82–83; Peterson, *Acts*, 235; Toussaint, "Acts," 2:367.

[22] Bock, *Acts*, 258; Joachim Jeremias, *Jerusalem in the Time of Jesus: An Investigation into Economic and Social Conditions During the New Testament Period*, trans. F. H. Cave and C. H. Cave (Philadelphia: Fortress Press, 1969), 131; Polhill, *Acts*, 180.

[23] Jacob Neusner, ed. *The Babylonian Talmud: A Translation and Commentary* (Peabody, MA: Hendrickson, 2011), in *Logos Library System* [CD–ROM], s.v. "b. B. Bat. 8B."

[24] Marcus Jastrow, A Dictionary of the Targumim, the Talmud Babli and Yerushalmi, and the Midrashic Literature (New York: G. P. Putnam's Sons, 1903), in Logos Library System [CD–ROM], s.v. "קוּפָּה," s.v. "תַּמְחוּי".

everyone, whether or not they were residents (b. B. Bat. 8B). The "charity fund" involved a weekly distribution of money sufficient for fourteen meals (m. Pe'a 8:7 F-H) and was for residents only (b. B. Bat. 8B).[25] Comparing these practices (b. B. Bat. 8B; m. Pe'a 8:7 F-H) and Acts 6, "τῇ διακονίᾳ τῇ καθημερινῇ" [the daily distribution] (Acts 6:2), we find they are similar to the soup kitchen, but "αἱ χῆραι αὐτῶν" [their widows] (Acts 6:1), is similar to the "charity fund," because the group mentioned is specifically restricted by the language to residents or members of the community. Consequently, the scholarly consensus is that, in Acts 6, the apostles were not strictly following the charity practices reflected in the Talmud, but rather, according to Jeremias, "these arrangements served as a *model* for the primitive Church" so that, as Polhill explains, the "Christian practice seems to have embraced elements of both Jewish systems."[26] If elements of both Jewish charity systems (the soup kitchen and the charity fund) were involved in Acts 6:1-2 and since the charity fund involved money and not food, then "τραπέζαις" [tables] necessarily refers to the "money lender's bench" or a "bank," and the passage involves a transfer of financial authority.

However, Capper argues that the Talmudic practice is too different from the description in Acts 6 and is too late to have been the custom in the first century.[27] Capper argues that the charity practices of the Essenes, as described by Philo (*Hypoth.* 11:10-11) and Hippolytus (*Haer.* 9.14), are closer to the practice described by the "τῇ διακονίᾳ τῇ καθημερινῇ" [the daily distribution] in Acts 6:2.[28] For example, Philo describes the Essenes charity practice:

> (11.10) Accordingly, each of these men, who differ so widely in their respective employments, when they have received their wages give them up to one person who is appointed as the universal steward and general manager; and he, when he has

---

[25] Jacob Neusner, ed. *The Mishnah: A New Translation* (New Haven, CT: Yale University Press, 1988), in *Logos Library System* [CD–ROM], s.v. "m. Pe'a 8:7 F–H."

[26] Emphasis added. Bock, *Acts*, 258; Jeremias, *Jerusalem of Jesus*, 131; Keener, *Acts 3:1–14:28*, K.l. 2:8764–65; Polhill, *Acts*, 180.

[27] Brian Capper, "The Palestinian Cultural Context of Earliest Christian Community of Goods," in *BAPS*, 350–51.

[28] Ibid., 352–53.

> received the money, immediately goes and purchases what is *necessary* and furnishes them with food in abundance, and all other things of which the life of mankind stands in *need.* (11.11) And those who live together and *eat at the same table are day after day* contented with the same things, being lovers of frugality and moderation, and averse to all sumptuousness and extravagance as a disease of both mind and body (Emphasis added).[29]

Capper claims that Philo's account of the Essenes' charitable practices and Acts 6 share in common an emphasis on meeting needs, a daily practice, and tables, where the tables (Acts 6:2) are the daily "table-fellowship" of Acts 2:46.[30] Even if Capper's rejection of the Talmudic evidence and comparison to the Essences are accepted, the Essene practice as described by Philo and Hippolytus still involve the authority to handle money.

Two points seem decisive in interpreting the term "τραπέζαις" [tables]. Regardless of whether the Talmudic or Essene charitable practice is compared to Acts 6, both involved money. Similarly to the description of the charitable practices of the Essenes, the Talmud explicitly indicates that even when it was only food that was being distributed, there were still circumstances in which money was involved and the "charity supervisors" had financial responsibilities and authority: "Along these same lines, charity supervisors who did not find poor folk among whom to distribute the beans that they have collected for the poor may sell the beans to others, but they do not sell it to themselves."[31] Additionally, when the term "διακονία" in the phrase, "τῇ διακονίᾳ τῇ καθημερινῇ" [the daily distribution], in Acts 6:2, is used elsewhere by Luke and Paul to describe the support given to the poor in Jerusalem, the context explicitly interprets the term as a reference to dealing with money (Acts 11:29; Rom. 15:31; 2 Cor. 8:4; 9:1, 12-13).[32] Therefore, in Acts 6:2 the phrase "διακονεῖν τραπέζαις" refers to "taking care of the money lender's bench" or a "bank" and even if it does not, the charity practices involved in the passage still indicate that a transfer of financial authority occurred to resolve the conflict over unmet needs.[33]

---

[29] Philo of Alexandria, *Hypth.* 11:10–11 "Hypothetica: Apology for the Jews," in *The Works of Philo: Complete and Unabridged* (Peabody, MA: Hendrickson, 1995), in *Logos Library System* [CD–ROM], 745–746.

[30] Capper, "Community of Goods," 352–53.

[31] Neusner, *Babylonian Talmud*, s.v. "b. B. Mes. 38A."

[32] Arndt, BDAG, s.v. "διακονία."

[33] Parsons, *Acts*, 83–84.

(4) *Transfer of Decision-Making Authority*: In Acts 6:3 and 5-6, as their response to the complaint, the apostles (OBCs) resolved the conflict by transferring decision-making authority for meeting the needs of the Hellenists (LBCs) to the Hellenists (LBCs). Two textual features indicate that responsibility or authority was transferred. In Acts 6:3, according to the BDAG, the term "καταστήσομεν," in the phrase "whom we will put in charge over this need," means "to assign someone a position of *authority*, appoint, put in charge."[34] Additionally, in Acts 6:6 the act of "laying on hands" was a symbolic act of commissioning that conferred or transferred authority to the Hellenists to discharge their responsibility of meeting the needs of the widows.[35]

One textual feature indicates that the authority was transferred to the Hellenists. In Acts 6:5, although Jews could have Greek names, there is a strong scholarly consensus that, since the seven names listed in the verse are Greek, that this ethnic attribute indicates that the authority to care for the widows was transferred to the Hellenists.[36] Therefore, the conflict over the unmet needs of the Hellenists (LBCs) by the Hebraists (OBCs) was resolved in part by transferring decision-making authority for the responsibility of meeting those needs from the Hebraists (OBCs) to the injured party, the Hellenists (LBCs).

In Acts 6:1-7, the transfer of financial and decision-making authority is an ecclesiastical rather than a spiritual-relational solution. The following section on "Supplemental and Implied Points" demonstrates that there are spiritual-relational elements in the passage. However, the main and explicit points of the solution in Acts 6:1-7 are ecclesiological rather than spiritual-relational. This emphasis means that, in the parallel ministry interpretation, Acts 6:1-7 is a valid analogy to the crisis of the immigrant church, because it stresses the ecclesiological aspect over the spiritual-relational aspect. Unlike parallel ministry's use of Acts 6:1-7, the

---

[34] Emphasis added. Arndt, BDAG, s.v. "καθίστημι/καθιστάνω." For a similar judgment see: Bock, *Acts*, 260; Peterson, *Acts*, 233; Parsons, *Acts*, 83; Polhill, *Acts*, 181.

[35] Bock, *Acts*, 262; Keener, *Acts 3:1–14:28*, K.l. 2:9292–93; Marshall, *Acts*, 127; Peterson, *Acts*, 235; Witherington, *Acts*, 251.

[36] Bock, *Acts*, 261; Bruce, *Acts*, 121; Keener, *Acts 3:1–14:28*, K.l. 2:9261; Marshall, *Acts*, 127; Parsons, *Acts*, 84; Peterson, *Acts*, 234; Polhill, *Acts*, 181; Toussaint, "Acts," 2:367; Witherington, *Acts*, 250.

alternative solutions are deficient, because their analogies are invalid due to the use of spiritual-relational passages to solve an ecclesiological issue.

(5) *One Church Interdependence*: Even though there was a transfer of financial and decision-making authority, the church still functioned as one church in interdependence (Acts 6:7). In Acts 6:7, the phrase "the disciples in Jerusalem," along with the later description of "the church at Jerusalem" (Acts 8:1; 11:22), indicate that, despite the transfer of financial and decision-making powers, the two groups (Hebraists and Hellenists) still constituted "one church," namely the Jerusalem church.[37] It is significant that the church of Acts 6:1-7 is still called the Jerusalem church (Acts 8:1; 11:22), even after the conflict. The church's name is significant because, in the NT, the term "ἐκκλησία" [church] frequently refers to the collective of house churches of an entire city (Acts 5:11; 13:1; 18:22; Rom. 16:1; 1 Cor. 1:2; 2 Cor. 1:1) or to individual house churches (Rom. 16:5; 1 Cor. 16:19; Col. 4:15). Furthermore, in the NT, the emphasis was placed the ethnic unity of the church (Eph. 2:11-22). However, the church could be subdivided by ethnic groups as when Paul speaks of "the churches of the Gentiles" (Rom. 16:4), and Luke distinguished synagogues in Jerusalem as being Hellenist, specifically "the Synagogue of the Freedmen" (Acts 6:9).[38] Since the NT could differentiate between synagogues (Acts 6:9) and churches (Rom. 16:4) based on ethnic identity when appropriate, but did not do so after the conflict in Acts 6:1 (i.e. church of the Hebraists and/or church of the Hellenists), then the name "church at Jerusalem" (Acts 6:7; 8:1; 11:22) indicates that the two groups still functioned as one church.

Immigrant churches frequently face conflict at later stages of their development when LBCs want to broaden the ethnic focus of the church beyond the OBC ethnic identity. An indication of this is when the church elects to change the name of the church or of the LBC congregation. Typically, immigrant churches are ethnically named in order to attract other OBCs, such as "First Chinese Baptist Church," "First

---

[37] Bock, *Acts*, 261; Polhill, *Acts*, 179.

[38] Arndt, BDAG, s.v. "ἐκκλησία;" G. W. Bromiley, "Church," in *ISBE*, ed. Geoffrey W. Bromiley (Grand Rapids: Wm. B. Eerdmans, 1988, in *Logos Library System* [CD–ROM], 1:693; Bruce, *Acts*, 124–25; G. N. Giles, "Church," in *Dictionary of the Later New Testament and Its Developments*, ed. Ralph P. Martin and Peter H. Davids (Downers Grove: InterVarsity, 1997), in *Logos Library System* [CD–ROM], s. v. "2.3.5 Church"; Keener, *Acts 3:1–14:28*, K.l. 2:9684–86; Peterson, *Acts*, 239–40; Polhill, *Act*, 184.

Korean Presbyterian," or "Evangelical Haitian Church." For example, Asian LBCs may want to change the church name from "Japanese Evangelical Church" to "Asian–American Community Church" in order to pursue Pan–Asians, or they may wish to change the name to "Covenant Life Church" in order to become multicultural. In this conflict, both OBCs and LBCs may note that the most common biblical example is that churches are named after their cities (Acts 8:1; 13:1; Rom. 16:1; 1 Cor. 1:2; 2 Cor. 1:1). Since the parallel ministry model allows for two interdependent congregations and focuses on spiritual unity in Christ (Eph. 4:1-6; John 4:23-24) rather than physical unity (John 4:19-21), then this model allows for the LBC congregation to call itself by a name different from the OBC congregation and yet still be one church. For example, the OBC congregation may call itself "Ethnic Church of the Immigrant Believer," while the LBC congregation calls itself "Community Church of (Insert City Name)."

Since the bilingual and separate service models typically focus on physical rather than spiritual unity by emphasizing one church, one budget, one board, and one vision, then they typically stress the necessity of having an ethnic church name to preserve their cultural identity and to stress that the church is one family. By stressing the OBC identity over the hybrid identity of LBC through the church name, these two models create an unhealthy dependence rather than the interdependence of Acts 6:1 and 3.

The church planting model allows for different church names through two independent churches, but does so by eliminating the interdependence of Acts 6:1 and 3 and by meeting the needs of some LBCs, while making immigrant churches less able to meet the needs of both OBCs and LBCs. Only the parallel ministry model allows for the one church interdependence of Acts 6:1 and 3 and for the expression of this interdependence through separate congregational names that reflect the primary NT practice of naming a church after the city in which it is located.

Acts 6:1 and 3 indicate that the two groups (Hebraists and Hellenists) functioned interdependently. In Acts 6:1, the Hellenistic Jews were depending on the Hebraic Jews to meet their needs, and in the solution implemented in Acts 6:3, the Hebraic Jews became dependent on the Hellenistic Jews either to meet the needs of all the widows (Hebraic and Hellenist) or just the Hellenistic widows.[39] Therefore, the transfer of financial and decision-making authority did not result in two *separate* churches or in two *independent* congregations, but rather there was still one church with two groups that functioned *interdependently*. One of the problems with the bilingual and separate services models is that they typically make LBCs dependent upon OBCs with the result that LBC needs go unmet. The church planting model makes some LBCs independent of OBCs with the result that the needs of some LBCs are more effectively met, but the needs of OBCs and some other LBCs are not met. Only the parallel ministry model provides an interdependent model rather than a dependent or independent model that most effectively meets the needs of both OBCs and LBCs.

(6) *Unbelievers Reached*: In Acts 6:7, "the increase in the number of disciples and priests" indicates that, as a result of the resolution of the conflict, the church was able to reach unbelievers from both groups.[40] In Acts 6:7, the opening "καὶ" at the head of the verse should be translated "and so" in order "to introduce a result that comes from [*sic*] what precedes."[41] The reason for this translation is that verse 7 is widely recognized, as stated by Longenecker, as being one of Luke's "summary statements or 'progress reports' (6:7; 9:31; 12:24; 16:5; 19:20; and 28:31)" which show "growth" (Acts 6:7; 12:24; 19:20) after or as the result of the resolution of a conflict or persecution.[42] Consequently, Luke's structure of "progress following from conflict/persecution" indicates that the church grew as a result of the resolution of the conflict between Hebraic and Hellenistic Jews.

---

[39] Keener has the seven Hellenist leaders caring for all the widows (Hebraic and Hellenist), while Capper and Marshall have them caring for only the Hellenist widows. Capper, "Community of Goods," 353–54; Keener, *Acts 3:1–14:28*, K.l. 2:9265–67; Marshall, *Acts*, 125.

[40] Marshall, *Acts*, 127; Peterson, *Acts*, 229.

[41] Arndt, BDAG, s.v. "καί;" Paul R. House, "Suffering and the Purpose of Acts," *JETS* 33, no. 3 (Sept 1990): 320–26, 330; John Peter Lange, ed. *A Commentary on the Holy Scriptures* (Bellingham, WA: Logos Bible Software, 2008), in *Logos Library Systerm* [CD–ROM], 105; R. C. H. Lenski, *The Interpretation of the Acts of the Apostles* (Minneapolis: Augsburg, 1961), in *Logos Library System* [CD–ROM], 248; Marshall, *Acts*, 127; Peterson, Acts, 229.

[42] Longenecker, *Acts*, 234; Bock, *Acts*, vii, 13, 264; Keener, *Acts 3:1–14:28*, K.l. 2:8526–27, 9305–06; Lenski, *Acts*, 248; Peterson, *Acts*, 229; Polhill, *Acts*, 344; Toussaint, "Acts," 2:368, Witherington, *Acts*, 74.

Furthermore, the passage indicates that the church grew by reaching people from both groups. In Acts 6:7, the term "disciples" is general, but since it is qualified as referring to those disciples being "in Jerusalem" and since Acts 6:1 has indicated that there were both Hebraic and Hellenistic Jews in Jerusalem, then both groups might be in view. Additionally, some historical facts relating to the priesthood indicate that both Hebraic and Hellenistic priests were reached with the Gospel in vs. 7. The priesthood that was getting saved (Acts 6:7) was rotating for service or taking turns to serve in the temple (1 Chr. 24:5-6; Luke 1:8-9; *C. Ap.* 2.108; *Ant.* 7.365).[43] Some of the priests were permanently living in Jerusalem (Luke 22:54; John 18:15) and others were returning to their homes in the Diaspora when their term of service was finished (Luke 1:23, 39-40).[44] Consequently, both Hebraic and Hellenistic priests were reached with the Gospel in vs. 7 as a result of the resolution of the conflict in Acts 6:1-6. Resolving conflict between OBCs and LBCs over unmet LBC needs does not guarantee success in evangelism, but Acts 6:7 indicates that transferring financial and decision-making authority in order to meet LBC needs allows for a church environment in which both groups may more effectively reach the lost.

Only the parallel ministry model through its transfer of financial and decision-making authority meets the needs of both OBCs and LBCs. The transfer of the two types of authority allows LBCs to create culturally relevant ministries within the same church as OBCs. The translation involved in bilingual ministry aimed at preserving OBC language and culture and the joint services of the separate service model aimed at preserving physical unity have proven to alienate LBCs and so contribute to the silent exodus. The independent LBC church of the church planting model only meets the needs of some LBCs, while the needs of other LBCs and OBCs go unmet.

---

[43] Joachim Jeremias, *Jerusalem of Jesus*, 198–200ff.; Craig S Keener, *The IVP Bible Background Commentary: New Testament* (Downers Grove: InterVarsity Press, 1993), in *Logos Library System* [CD–ROM], s. v. "Acts 6:7;" Lee I. Levine, *Jerusalem: Portrait of the City in the Second Temple Period (538 B.C.E.–70 C.E.)* (Philadelphia: Jewish Publication Society, 2002), 360.

[44] Ibid.

Supplemental and Implied Points

The following five additional points include elements that are supplemental to the basic outline of parallel ministry and/or are only implied by Acts 6:1-7.

(7) *Parallel Meetings*: In Acts 6:1, the Hebraists (OBCs) and Hellenists (LBCs) were likely meeting in separate houses for worship as evidenced by significant biblical and extra-biblical evidences (archeological and manuscript evidence). There are at least five evidences which indicate that the Hebraic Jews and Hellenistic Jews were likely meeting in separate houses or parallel meetings for worship. First, in Acts 6:1 the fact that the Hebraists and Hellenists are listed as separate cultural-linguistic groups that were in conflict with each other suggests that they were meeting separately for worship in their respective languages, possibly due to the historical cultural tensions (1 Macc. 1:11-15) that are known to have existed between the two groups.[45] Second, the fact that the Hebraists and Hellenists are listed separately (Acts 6:1) in conjunction with the fact that the early church met in private houses with limited seating capacity (Rom. 16:5; 1 Cor. 16:19; Col. 4:15; Phlm. 2) suggests that the Hebraic Jews and Hellenistic Jews naturally divided themselves among cultural-linguistic lines in the respective house churches.[46] Third, the Tosefta (t. Meg. 3.6 [224]) and Talmud (b. Meg. 26a; y. Meg. 3[2]:6; y. Meg. 73d [39-41]) indicate that a Hellenistic synagogue existed in Jerusalem at the time of Acts 6 and so it is likely that, just as Christian Jews followed the order of worship of Jewish synagogues (Luke 4:14-30), they also followed the example of separate Hebraic and Hellenistic worship services.[47] Fourth, there is the archeological evidence of the

---

[45] Bruce, *Acts*, 120; Marshall, *Acts*, 126; Longenecker, *Acts*, 329; Toussaint, "Acts," 2:367.

[46] Bruce, *Acts*, 120; Marshall, *Acts*, 126; R. P. Martin, "Worship and Liturgy," in *Dictionary of the Later New Testament and Its Developments*, ed. Ralph P. Martin and Peter H. Davids (Downers Grove: InterVarsity, 1997), in *Logos Library System* [CD–ROM], s.v. "5. The Rome–Asia Minor Axis."

[47] Keener, *Acts 3:1–14:28*, K.l. 2:9651–59; Martin, "Worship and Liturgy," s.v. "5. The Rome–Asia Minor Axis;" Marshall, *Acts*, 126; Peterson, *Acts*, 239–40; Polhill, *Act*, 184; Rainer Reisner, "Synagogues in Jerusalem," in *BAPS*, ed. Richard Bauckham, vol. 4 of The Book of Acts in Its First Century Setting (Grand Rapids: William B. Eerdmans 1995), 188–89; Emil Schürer, "Alexandrians in Jerusalem," in *The Jewish Encyclopedia*, ed. Isidore Singer (New York: Funk & Wagnalls, 1906), 371–72; R. S. Wallace, "Lord's Supper (Eucharist)," in *ISBE*, ed. Geoffrey W. Bromiley (Grand Rapids: Wm. B. Eerdmans, 1988), in *Logos Library System* [CD–ROM], 3:167.

"Theodotus inscription," a ten-line dedicatory inscription for a synagogue written in Greek, carved in limestone, and found in 1913. This inscription demonstrates that the Hellenists had a synagogue in Jerusalem, and like the Talmudic evidence, this fact indicates that the Hebraic and Hellenistic Jewish Christians met separately for worship.[48] Fifth, since it is common to understand the "Synagogue of the Freedmen" in Acts 6:9 as a Hellenistic synagogue meeting separately from the Hebraic synagogue in Jerusalem, then similarly to the Talmudic evidence and "Theodotus inscription," this fact indicates that the Hebraic and Hellenistic Jewish Christians met separately for worship.[49]

Through its separate worship services, the parallel ministry model allows OBCs and LBCs to each have culturally relevant worship in their respective languages. The single bilingual worship service creates an atmosphere in which neither the needs of OBCs or LBCs are fully met and whichever group receives the translation feels underappreciated. While the separate service model allows for culturally relevant worship much like the parallel ministry model, it tends to make LBCs dependent upon OBCs and lacks other features of parallel ministry such as two budgets, boards, and visions that help minimize LBC alienation and the LBC feeling of disenfranchisement from church ownership. The church planting model also allows for separate OBC and LBC culturally relevant worship services, but does so at the expense of OBCs and LBCs who stay in the immigrant church.

(8) *Control over Staffing*: In Acts 6:2-6, while the apostles/Hebraists (OBCs) took the initiative to resolve the problem so that the Hellenist's needs would be met, the whole church participated in the solution so that the Hellenists (LBCs) retained control over their staffing and leadership. In Acts 6:1-2, the Hellenists called attention to the

---

48 Keener, *Acts 3:1–14:28*, K.l. 2:9634–51; Marshall, *Acts*, 126; Peterson, *Acts*, 239–40; Polhill, *Act*, 184; Reisner, "Synagogues," 192–200, 204–06.

49 In vs. 9, there is dispute over how many synagogues the Greek grammar indicates, with suggestions ranging from one to five. However, most scholars accept that there was one synagogue attended by Jews from the various places of the Diaspora mention in the verse. Keener, *Acts 3:1–14:28*, K.l. 2:9684–86; Marshall, *Acts*, 126; Peterson, *Acts*, 239–40; Polhill, *Act*, 184; Reisner, "Synagogues," 204–06; Schürer, "Alexandrians," 371–72.

problem by "complaining" about their unmet needs (vs. 1), but since the apostles were the ones who "called to themselves the community of disciples" (vs. 2), then it was the Hebraists who took the initiative to solve the problem, not the Hellenists.[50] This textual point is a significant example to the contemporary immigrant church, because chapter 1 indicated that, since typically OBCs are the parents of the LBCs, they have the power in the immigrant church. As the ones in power, OBCs have the responsibility to imitate the example of the apostles and initiate the necessary changes to meet the needs of LBCs in their churches. OBC initiation of the solution is important, not only because of the apostles' example in Acts 6:2, but also because, as chapter 1 indicated, LBCs are often viewed by OBCs as being disrespectful when they complain and/or attempt to initiate the solution themselves. However, even though the apostles initiated the process, they did not control it.

The whole church participated in the solution so that the Hellenists (LBCs) retained control over their staffing. In Acts 6:2-3 and 5-6, the phrases, "the community of disciples" (vs. 2), "brothers, you select" (vs. 3), "in the opinion of the whole community" (vs. 5), and "they placed before" (vs. 6) indicate that the Hellenists participated in selecting their own leaders and that the Hebraists did not choose for them.[51] Furthermore, Bruce claims that the list of seven Greek names (Acts 6:5) implies that these men "were probably the recognized leaders of the Hellenists in the church."[52] If so, then not only did the apostles and Hebraists approve of the leaders selected by the whole church (Acts 6:6), but in the selection process, the Hebraic Jews possibly approved the leaders already recognized by the Hellenists as leaders (Acts 6:5-6).

This Hebraist approval of leaders already recognized by the Hellenists (Acts 6:5-6) is particularly important in light of the fact that the apostles set the qualifications for leadership (Acts 6:3) in view of the differences in perception of spiritual maturity between OBCs and LBCs presented in chapter 1. In Acts 6:3, the apostles set three qualifications for the leaders to be selected by the congregation, namely that they be (1)

---

[50] For a similar judgment see: Land, *Diffusion of Ecclesiastical Authority*, K.l. 5593–95; Peterson, *Acts*, 232; Polhill, *Acts*, 180–81.

[51] Bock, *Acts*, 260; Bruce, *Acts*, 122; Keener, *Acts 3:1–14:28*, K.l. 2:8967–68, 8976–77, 9095–98; Longenecker, *Acts*, 331; Parsons, *Acts*, 84; Peterson, *Acts*, 233, 235; Polhill, *Acts*, 180; Witherington, *Acts*, 249.

[52] Bruce, *Acts*, 121; see also: Capper, "Community of Goods," 354; Keener, *Acts 3:1–14:28*, K.l. 2:8944–46.

"full of the Spirit," (2) "full of wisdom," and (3) "have a good reputation" for the first two qualities.[53] The importance of the three qualifications for leadership, which imply spiritual maturity, cannot be understated. These qualifications are more of a spirutual–relational issue than an eccelsastical concern and are only discussed in a limited manner as they impact the church's structure. However, some, like Lowe, may see the qualifications as an ecclesiastical concern. For example, Lowe claims that the spiritual maturity of the Hellenists (LBCs) is likely a fruit of the Hebraist's (OBC) ministry. If true, then this fruit implies that the transfer of decision making authority from OBCs to spiritually mature LBC leaders is part of a discipleship process necessary for the spiritual development of the LBC congregation.[54]

In Acts 6:5-6, the apostles/Hebraists (OBCs) accepted the Hellenists' (LBCs') evaluation or judgment of which Hellenists (LBCs) were qualified or spiritually mature to be in leadership. Since chapter 1 demonstrated that OBCs and LBCs have different cultural perceptions of spiritual maturity in such a way that OBC leaders often do not perceive LBCs to be qualified for leadership, then the apostolic/Hebraic acceptance of the Hellenist's recognized leaders (Acts 6:5-6) is a powerful example for OBCs to allow LBCs to retain a great deal of control over their staffing decisions. The following examples illustrate how differing cultural perceptions of spiritual maturity in regard to wisdom (Acts 6:3) can impact qualification for church leadership.

In some Asian cultures, OBCs may find it wise to lie in order to allow others to save face or to avoid being publicly shamed. On the other hand, many LBCs may find lying to be contrary to the character of God and so it is considered unwise or foolish (1 Sam. 15:29; Col. 3:9–10; Titus 1:2). Under these circumstances, OBCs may find LBCs unwise, spiritually immature, and disrespectful who are unwilling to lie in order to allow their elders to save face. In contrast, LBCs may believe their own actions to be in obedience to God and feel that their elders' insistence to perceived unethical or cultural traditions is wrong. This creates an atmosphere where

---

[53] Toussaint, "Acts," 2:367; similarly: Bock, *Acts*, 260; Polhill, *Acts*, 181. See also: Arndt, BDAG, s. v. "μαρτυρέω."

[54] Curtis Lowe to Ronald M. Rothenberg, "Discussion of Parallel Ministry," 25 October 2014, FaceTime.

the LBCs may disobey their parents' wishes openly and even blatantly. On the other hand, OBCs may find LBCs who explicitly disobey their parents to be foolishly in violation of the biblical imperative to obey/honor one's parents (Ex. 20:12; Eph. 6:1–3; Col. 3:20). In these situations, OBCs may find LBCs who are attempting to express deep faith and dedication to God to lack wisdom and spiritual maturity and thus are unacceptable leaders. These examples illustrate that the cultural norms of any group can be mistaken for spiritual standards such as wisdom by both OBCs and LBCs. The Bible challenges everyone to strive to transcend human cultural values by seeking a Kingdom culture conformed the character of God as expressed in His Word (Rom. 8:29; Eph. 5:1; 2 Tim. 3:16–17).

In contemporary application, both the stage of church growth and the type of congregational polity (Baptist, Presbyterian, Congregational, etc.) will impact the details of the process for selecting and approving LBC leadership. For example, if OBCs have wisely decided to obey Acts 6 and implement parallel ministry at an early stage of church growth, then the LBCs may be too young (infants or small children) to have much participation in the process of their leadership selection. However, if as is usually the case, parallel ministry as described in Acts 6 is discovered and implemented when LBCs are older (youth, young adults, adults), then Acts 6 implies that OBCs are to follow the example of the apostles/Hebraists by respecting LBC staffing/leadership decisions despite differences in the perception of spiritual maturity. Acts 6:2-6 indicates that, while the apostles/Hebraists (OBCs) took the initiative to resolve the problem so that the Hellenist's needs would be met, the whole church participated in the solution so that the Hellenists (LBCs) retained control over their staffing.

(9) *Spiritual-Relational Aspect*: Both the Hebraic (OBC) and Hellenistic (LBC) Jewish Christians displayed spiritual-relational dispositions or attitudes that allowed for the solution (Acts 6:2, 5). Despite the fact that the primary focus of this book is the ecclesiastical aspect of the immigrant church crisis rather than the spiritual-relational aspect—since the two solutions must be implemented together—it is important to briefly note the presence of the spiritual-relational aspect in the primary passage on parallel ministry. In Acts 6:1-2, when the Hellenists called attention to the problem by "complaining" about their unmet needs (vs. 1), the apostles responded favorably by proposing a solution (vs. 2) rather than placing blame, denying the problem, seeking retribution against their

accusers, or being paternalistic in solving the problem.[55] In Acts 6:5, likewise, the fact that the apostle's proposed solution "was pleasing to the whole community" demonstrates that both the Hebraists and Hellenists also had spiritual-relational dispositions or attitudes that allowed for the solution (Acts 6:1-6).[56] Therefore, Acts 6:2 and 5 demonstrates that in order for parallel ministry to be implemented, both OBCs and LBCs must imitate the mature spiritual-relational dispositions, attitudes, or Christian character exemplified in the passage.

Parallel ministry challenges both OBCs and LBCs toward spiritual maturity. For example, OBCs are challenged to subordinate their desire to preserve their language and culture (Col. 2:6-8) to the need for LBCs to be saved (Matt. 28:18-20) by allowing LBCs to create a culturally relevant ministry (Acts 6:1). Relinquishing power through the transfer of financial and decision-making authority means that OBCs must have courage (Deut. 31:6-7) to allow LBCs to make mistakes and patience (Gal. 5:22) and self-control (Gal. 5:23) to allow LBCs to shape their ministry in ways that contradict OBC culture, but are biblically acceptable. Likewise, LBCs are challenged to have the courage (Josh. 2:6-9) to strive toward financial interdependence, the wisdom (Prov. 1:7) to strive for interdependence rather than independence (1 Tim. 5:8), and the discipline (Gal. 5:23) and diligence (1 Tim. 4:15) to take responsibility for their ministry's operations and direction rather than continuing to dependently rely solely on OBC support and safety. In contrast to parallel ministry, both bilingual worship and separate services allow OBCs to sacrifice courage (Deut. 31:6-7) for cultural comfort (Col. 2:6-8) and LBCs to sacrifice maturity (Heb. 5:14) for dependence. Similarly, the church planting model trades interdependent patience with (Gal. 5:22) and love for (1 Cor. 13:13) OBCs and new LBCs for the comfort and in some ways selfish pleasures (Gal. 5:20; 2 Tim. 3:2; Heb. 11:25) of an independent church.

(10) *Different Visions*: The Hebraists (OBCs) and Hellenists (LBCs) remained one church as they successfully reached the lost of both

---

55 Land, *Diffusion of Ecclesiastical Authority*, K.l. 3667–70ff.; Longenecker, *Acts*, 330–32.

56 Keener, *Acts 3:1–14:28*, K.l. 2:8690–91, 8713–17, 9095–98, 9101–04; Longenecker, *Acts*, 330–32; Witherington, *Acts*, 250.

groups, while pursuing different visions (Acts 6:1, 7). In Acts 6:1, since the Hebraists neglected the needs of the Hellenists while the Hellenists were concerned about the needs in their own community, the two groups likely had different ministry focuses or visions. A further reaching, but valid implication of this neglect and unmet needs divided along cultural-linguistic lines in the passage is that the Hebraic Jews were focused on the ministry to Hebraic Jews, while the Hellenistic Jews were focused on the ministry to Hellenistic Jews. In support of such a division of visions, in Galatians 2:1 and 8-10, the leaders of the Jerusalem church (James, Peter, and John) are explicitly said to have a mission, focus, or vision to reach the Jews rather than the Gentiles.[57] Since the Hellenistic Jews had much in common with the Gentiles and, unlike the leaders of the Jerusalem church (Gal. 2:1, 8-10), had a vision to reach out to Greeks (Acts 11:19-20), then it is possible that the vision of the Hebraic Jews in Jerusalem did not extend to or at least strongly incorporate Hellenistic Jews. If one accepts that the Hebraic (OBCs) and Hellenistic (LBCs) Jews had different ministry visions based on their different focuses on meeting needs (Acts 6:1) and canonical evidence (Acts 11:19-20; Gal. 2:1, 8-10), then it should be remembered that, despite these different visions, "One Church Interdependence" and "Unbelievers Reached" demonstrated that the Jerusalem church remained one church and reached the lost of both groups (Acts 6:7). Therefore, (Acts 6:1, 7) implies that a church may consist of two parallel congregations, OBC and LBC, with distinct ministry visions to reach different groups, yet remain one interdependent church.

In Acts 6:1 and 7, the implied point that the two groups, OBCs and LBCs, had separate visions is one feature of parallel ministry that is crucial for solving the crisis of the immigrant church. Typically, in immigrant churches, OBCs want to reach other OBCs and their homeland, and they expect LBCs to have the same concerns. LBCs are often expected to become missionaries to their homeland. These types of OBC ministry expectations normally alienate LBCs who are primarily concerned with reaching other LBCs and frequently have a concern to share the Gospel with people from the host culture and other assimilated cultural groups living in the host culture. Since 1.5, second, and

[57] James D. G. Dunn, *The Epistle to the Galatians*, BNTC (London: Continuum, 1993), in *Logos Library System* [CD–ROM], 107, 111; Timothy George, *Galatians*, vol. 30, NAC (Nashville: Broadman & Holman, 1994), in *Logos Library System* [CD–ROM], 162; Richard N. Longenecker, *Galatians*, vol. 41, WBC (Dallas: Word, 1998), in *Logos Library System* [CD–ROM], 55, 58.

succeeding generation LBCs simultaneously identify with and are alienated by both the host and OBC cultures, many times LBCs will choose to reach OBCs or become missionaries to their homeland. Normally, LBCs will be more open to these OBCs oriented ministries when they feel that the decision to pursue such ministries is their own decision rather than the result of meeting OBC expectations. Since the OBC homeland, immigrant OBCs, LBCs, the host culture, and other assimilated groups living in the host culture all need to be reached with the Gospel (Matt. 28:18-20), then the parallel ministry feature from Acts 6:1 and 7 of allowing OBCs and LBCs to pursue their own visions most adequately meets the needs of everyone.

Certainly, the bilingual and separate service models may also incorporate the practice of having separate visions for both groups as the church planting model does. However, allowing for separate visions alone does not in itself overcome the other problems with these three alternatives to parallel ministry. Furthermore, as the three alternative models are actually practiced, they do not allow for separate visions with the intention of meeting the needs of both groups as only parallel ministry does by drawing on Acts 6:1 and 7. The bilingual and separate service models typically focus on physical rather than spiritual unity by emphasizing one church, one budget, one board, and one vision. The church planting model allows for different visions, but does so by meeting the needs of some LBCs, while making immigrant churches less able to meet the needs of both OBCs and LBCs. Only parallel ministry from Acts 6:1 and 7 allows for different visions with the intention of meeting the needs of everyone.

(11) *Equal Authority*: The Hebraic (OBC) and Hellenistic (LBC) Jewish Christian leaders had equal authority after the disciples' solution was implemented (Acts 6:2-4, 6). In Acts 6:2-4 and 6, the facts that the apostles delegated their former area of ministry to the Hellenists (Acts 4:34-37; 5:2) and that they transferred the decision-making authority to the Hellenists in an unqualified manner implies that the Hellenist leaders were given equal authority to that of the apostles/Hebraist leaders in their ministry area.[58] On this idea of equal authority, Land claims, "In

[58] For a similar judgment see: Parsons, *Acts*, 84; Peterson, *Acts*, 235. Capper makes a different argument, but its result is a stitution where both groups have equal authority. Capper, "Community of Goods," 353–54.

the Jerusalem church, as in many Greco-Roman religions, the structure is based on differentiation of tasks, not upon hierarchical subordination and supervision....The language of v. 4 implies that the Twelve retain no control over the work assigned to the Seven."[59] Therefore, the Hebraic (OBC) and Hellenistic (LBC) Jewish Christian leaders had equal authority after the disciple's solution was implemented (Acts 6:2-4, 6).

Only the parallel ministry model allows for the type of equal authority in Acts 6:2-4 and 6 which resolves the various concerns raised in chapter 1. In bilingual and separate service models, despite the presence of LBCs on the church board, OBCs typically retain financial and decision-making authority. This retention of authority in these models leads to a cycle of tension. The church planting model has a type of equal authority, but achieves it only by removing some LBCs from the immigrant church so that the needs of both OBCs and some LBCs go unmet. The equal authority achieved through parallel leadership (co-pastors and separate boards) alleviates OBC pastoral fears that they will be replaced and causes LBCs to take responsibility for their ministry. In turn, this structure allows OBCs who lost the prestige of social position from their home country to retain their church leadership and allows LBCs to create a culturally relevant ministry that meets their needs while meeting the OBC need to have their children taken care of.

A Normative Definition of Parallel Ministry

While proponents of the separate service model do not provide a consistent definition of parallel ministry (see chapter 5), the preceding exegesis of Acts 6 allows for a uniform and authoritative definition of parallel ministry. True parallel ministry may be defined by the elements drawn from Acts 6:1-7:

1. A *valid analogy* exists between the passage and the contemporary situation in the immigrant church (Acts 6:1). According to Acts 6:1-7, parallel ministry must consist of both an ecclesiastical structure (Acts 6:2-7) and spiritual-relational elements (Acts 6:2, 5).
2. *Cultural relevance* (meeting of needs, Acts 6:1).
3. Financial authority (Acts 6:2).
4. Decision-making authority (Acts 6:3-6).

[59] Land, Diffusion of Ecclesiastical Authority, K.l. 3683–84, 3687–88.

5. *Interdependence* (Acts 6:7). These last four main structural components function in conjunction with the following supplemental points implied by Acts 6:1-7.
6. OBCs and LBCs meet separately for worship in *parallel meetings* (Acts 6:1, 9).
7. LBCs retain a large measure of *control over their staffing and leaders* (Acts 6:2-6).
8. OBCs and LBCs have *different visions* for ministry (Acts 6:1; Gal. 2:1, 8-10).
9. OBC and LBC leaders have *equal authority* (Acts 6:2-4, 6).
10. Implementation and maintenance of the parallel ministry structure in Acts 6:1-7 requires and presupposes the *spiritual-relational* dispositions, attitudes, and Christian character implied by the passage (Acts 6:2, 5).
11. And results in a church atmosphere that allows for effective *outreach to both OBC and LBC unbelievers* (Acts 6:7).

Therefore, according to Acts 6:1-7, parallel ministry exists when favorable spiritual-relational conditions occur such that OBCs transfer financial and decision-making authority to LBCs so that they may create a culturally relevant interdependent ministry that meets needs.

While the main structural components and supplemental points provide a broad outline for parallel ministry, it is possible to make some more specific applications to the contemporary immigrant church. The application of these main structural components and supplemental points to the contemporary immigrant church results in:

1. Co-pastors rather than a hierarchy (often expressed as team leadership).
2. Parallel services.
3. Parallel boards.
4. Parallel budgets.
5. Separate visions.
6. Interdependence in terms of OBC children attending the LBC children's ministry, Sunday school, youth group, and other fellowships.
7. Interdependence in the form of OBCs financially supporting LBCs early in ministry and LBCs supporting OBCs later in ministry.

8. Interdependence through some joint culturally relevant activities not including joint services.

To gain a better understanding of what parallel ministry looks like, see "Table 1: Partial Parallel Ministry Agreement from an Actual Immigrant Church" on the next page.

Table 1: Partial Parallel Ministry Agreement from an Actual Immigrant Church

"Form" of Unity	Financial Authority	Decision-Making
1. No joint services were accepted and started immediately.	1. LBC Ministry collects their own offering, deposits it in their account. LBC ministry gives the church as a whole a "lump sum" on a monthly basis to help cover all the "joint costs:" gas, electric, water, trash, phone, copy machine, property tax, church minivan, gardener, alarm fees, 10% to the presbytery, missions budget, etc.	1. The church now has "one board" and "two meetings" since this was ruled not to violate the bylaws. The separate "board meetings" have "generally" all the responsibility and authorities of the "joint" board as outlined in the bylaws with the exceptions noted below that were ruled to violate the bylaws.
2. Separate baptism ceremonies. (Communion was already separate and remains so.)	2. In order to accurately calculate #1, the LBC and OBC treasurers got together and confirmed all church expenses.	2. There are 2 scheduled joint board meetings a year (Nov. and May), with more as needed, to discuss joint issues: budget, facilities, other financial issues, etc.
(3. See note below on joint activities.)	3. After #2 the board mutually agreed on a figure for the above "lump sum" in #1 that was manageable for the LBC offering amount and fair for the church.	3. LBC board member nominations to come from the LBC board but to be approved by the joint board in accordance with the bylaws.
	4. The LBC ministry and OBC ministry used the same accounting software to share records.	4. Elections of board members still done in one congregational meeting.
	5. LBC ministry writes these checks: reimbursements, LBC Pastor's pay check, 401K, insurance, health care, and dental (And for other future LBC staff.).	5. Voting on LBC Pastor's contract renewal done in joint board and congregation as in bylaws.
	6. The overall "church budget" is not changed since the "bottom line" is not changed. The changes are only a matter of who keeps track of the money and which account it is kept in.	6. Separate board/congregational meetings for budget approval. The joint board will discuss the proposed budgets before approval in the Nov. joint meeting.
	7. The board officially approved these changes and put them in the meeting minutes.	7. The "board meetings" will exchange meeting minutes for more communication. LBCs are responsible to translate OBC minutes into English.
	8. A feedback time was scheduled at the next annual planning meeting.	8. Hiring and firing of LBC staff members to be handled by LBCs but approved by the joint board to uphold bylaws.
	9. These financial changes were implemented at the OBC request for the starting date.	

Note: The LBC ministry still desires to change the bylaws so that the following items under the "Decision-Making" column can be amended to obtain a "true" parallel ministry: 1. Separate boards not just "meetings," 3. Boards nominate and approve members separately, 4. Elections done in separate congregational meetings, 5 & 8. Staff issues decided in board of that congregation. 6. Budget approved in separate congregational meetings, and 11. A change from a Senior Pastor to a Co-pastor system. (After this agreement was implemented, the LBC ministry felt the freedom to take the initiative to plan and organize community outreach activities that included OBC participation. The activities went well and both ministries seemed pleased with the outcomes.)

It may be unclear how some of these specific applications follow from the broad outline of parallel ministry derived from Acts 6:1-7 and why they are significant to immigrant church ministry, so the remainder of this section will provide some further explanation.

Exactly how the contemporary application of the transfer of financial and decision-making authority and how the implication of equal authority in Acts 6 results in co-pastors and why this is significant for the immigrant church requires some clarification. As explained in chapter 1, since OBCs view the church as an extended hierarchal family in which the OBC pastor is the patriarchal leader, it is difficult for OBCs to transfer decision-making authority (Acts 6:2-4) to LBCs and to do so in a manner that bestows equal authority to LBC leaders (Acts 6:2-6). However, the image of the church as a family, which OBCs emphasize for cultural reasons, is only one of at least ninety-six biblical metaphors used to describe the church.[60] The image of the church as a family is used primarily in Scripture to instruct the church on how its members should relate to each other (1 Tim. 5:1-2; 1 Pet. 3:8; 1 John 3:10-11) and particularly with regard to their unity (Eph. 2:19; 3:14-15; Heb. 2:11), not as a metaphor to guide the church's leadership structure.[61]

A metaphor which does guide the church's leadership structure is that of a flock of sheep with the corresponding image of a shepherd as the church's leader (1 Pet 5:2-4).[62] In 1 Peter 5:4 and Hebrews 13:20, Christ's titles respectively as the "ἀρχιποίμενος" [chief shepherd] and the "τὸν ποιμένα τὸν μέγαν" [the great shepherd] have traditionally been taken to imply that elders serve as "ὑπηρέτης" [under-shepherds] (Acts 20:28; 26:16; 1 Cor. 4:1; 1 Pet. 5:1-2) or assistant shepherds to Christ.[63] In

---

[60] Minear, who seems to have written the definitive work on the images of the church in the Bible, lists ninety–six images and claims that there are up to a hundred images. Paul S. Minear, *Images of the Church in the New Testament*, Kindle ed., The New Testament Library (Philadelphia: Westminster, 2004), K.l. 68–69, 695–96, 4103, 5108.

[61] Ibid., K.l. 3225–26, 3287–88, 3293.

[62] Ibid., K.l. 1707–13, 1737–39, 1749–51.

[63] Paul Ellingworth, *The Epistle to the Hebrews: A Commentary on the Greek Text*, NIGTC (Grand Rapids: W.B. Eerdmans, 1993), in *Logos Library System* [CD–ROM], 729; James M. Freeman, *Manners & Customs of the Bible* (North Brunswick, NJ: Bridge–Logos, 1998), in *Logos Library System* [CD–ROM], 547; Karen H. Jobes, *1 Peter*, BECNT (Grand Rapids: Baker Academic, 2005), in *Logos Library System* [CD–ROM], 304; Timothy S. Laniak, *Shepherds after My Own Heart: Pastoral Traditions and Leadership in the Bible*, ed. D. A. Carson, New Studies in Biblical Theology, vol.

practical application and in contrast to the hierarchy of the patriarchal family, the transfer of equal decision-making authority in a non-hierarchal manner (Acts 6:2-6) in relation to the image of all elders serving as equal under-shepherds of Christ's flock means that the OBC and LBC pastors serve as co-pastors.[64]

Through the implementation of equal authority through co-pastors (Acts 6:2-6; 20;28; 1 Pet. 5:2-4; Heb. 13:20), only the parallel ministry model effectively resolves the particular pastoral concerns expressed in chapter 1 and other practical ministerial tensions typically found in immigrant churches. In the description of the details of the crisis in chapter 1, some OBC pastors feared that bilingual-bicultural LBCs leaders would replace them. Since the bilingual and separate service models view the church as a hierarchy, then they only allow for a single patriarchal leader/senior pastor. These structures necessitate that only an OBC or LBC may be the senior church leader and make the OBC fear of replacement a legitimate concern. The church planting model alleviates this fear by meeting the needs of some LBCs, while leaving the needs of other LBCs and OBCs unmet. Only the parallel ministry model effectively relieves the OBC concern of replacement by establishing co-pastors to lead their respective congregations.[65]

---

20 (Downers Grove: InterVarsity, 2006), 225, 232–34; Minear, *Images of the Church*, K.l. 1711–13.

[64] Recently this sort of idea has been promoted as "team leadership," but without a sufficient biblical basis, although Cladis appeals to Trinitarian theology for support. George Cladis, *Leading the Team–Based Church: How Pastors and Church Staffs Can Grow Together into a Powerful Fellowship of Leaders* (San Francisco: Jossey–Bass, 1999), 3–10; Robert Webber, *The Younger Evangelicals: Facing the Challenges of the New World* (Grand Rapids: Baker Books, 2002), 151–53; Lovett H. Weems, Jr., *Church Leadership: Vision, Team, Culture, and Integrity* Revised ed. (Nashville: Abingdon, 2010), 55–79. Although some argue from 1 Timothy 5:17 that elders have different roles, the image of under–shepherd still implies an equality of leadership, particularly when interpreted in light of the body–metaphor (1 Cor 12:12–26). Minear argues that the various images of the church are interrelated and that "strategic inferences may be drawn from that interweaving." Minear, *Images of the Church*, 4222–24 ff.

[65] Acts 6:2-6; 20:28; 1 Pet. 5:2-4; Heb. 13:20.

Another set of practical pastoral concerns is only effectively resolved by the parallel ministry model's implementation of equal authority through co-pastors.[66] The patriarchal-hierarchal view of church leadership involved in the bilingual and separate service models creates tension between the OBC senior pastor and LBC associate/assistant pastor in at least two ways. First, the LBC pastor is accountable to and required to follow the ministerial directions of a leader with whom they often cannot (effectively) communicate due to language and cultural differences and who frequently does not understand the needs of the LBC ministry. Second, there is normally the expectation that the OBC pastor will disciple the LBC pastor, but language and cultural differences as well as different visions and philosophies of ministry make such a discipleship relationship impractical and ineffective. The church planting model does alleviate these tensions, but does so through the undesirable solution of creating a separate LBC church that only meets the needs of some LBCs while leaving the needs of LBCs and OBCs in the immigrant church unmet. By implementing co-pastors with equal authority who report to their respective boards, only the parallel ministry model most effectively resolves the pastoral tensions inherent in the other ministry models while still meeting the needs of both OBCs and LBCs.[67]

Exactly how the contemporary application of the transfer of financial and decision-making authority in Acts 6 results in parallel boards and budgets also requires some clarification. With regard to parallel boards, in the same way that the whole church only met to deal with special issues that impacted everyone (Acts 1:23; 6:2-3, 5-6; 11:22; 12, 22; 15:4), but individual leaders dealt with daily operations (Acts 2:45; 4:34-5:2; 15:36-41), so the joint board meeting of contemporary immigrant churches would likely be held only once or twice a year to discuss joint issues such as facilities, financial needs, and joint activities.[68]

By implementing separate boards to address daily operations and joint boards to handle special issues that impact everyone, only the parallel ministry model effectively deals with many of the practical

---

[66] Acts 6:2-6; 20:28; 1 Pet. 5:2-4; Heb. 13:20.

[67] Acts 6:2-6; 20:28; 1 Pet. 5:2-4; Heb. 13:20.

[68] Richard Bauckham, "James and the Jerusalem Church," in *BAPS*, 427–28; Land, *Diffusion of Ecclesiastical Authority*, K.l. 3703–05, 4872–78, 5595–96, 5610–11; Peterson, *Acts*, 422, 436; Longenecker, *Acts*, 331; Polhill, *Acts*, 180, 326, 328. Bruce dissents from this interpretation and claims that while the whole church was present, only the leaders made the decisions in Acts 15. Bruce, *Acts*, 289.

tensions that occur in the bilingual and separate service models, while still meeting the needs of both OBCs and LBCs, unlike the church planting model.[69]

The separate boards for daily operations of parallel ministry address the issue of relevance that alienates LBCs from the board.[70] In a typical OBC church, the LBCs typically get one line-item on the board agenda to report to the OBCs about their ministry or to make financial requests. This LBC report/request commonly only briefly interrupts OBC discussions of their routine ministry items, conducted in the OBC language, and which have little to no relevance to the LBC ministry. LBC leaders then need to conduct a separate meeting from the board to discuss items involving their ministry. With parallel board meetings, each group discusses issues relating to their respective daily ministry operations separately and only meets periodically to discuss issues that pertain to both groups in the joint board meetings. Through the use of separate boards, parallel ministry makes board meetings more effective for both OBCs and LBCs and makes such meetings relevant for LBCs so that they are not alienated from serving on the board.

The separate and joints boards of the parallel ministry model address the issue of communication that alienates LBCs from serving on the board. Just as the Hebraic Jews likely were bilingual, speaking Aramaic and Greek, but most of the Hellenists spoke little or no Aramaic (Acts 6:1) so that communication between the two groups probably occurred in Greek, so the joint board would be held in the LBC language to facilitate communication.[71] Depending on the actual language proficiencies in specific congregations, joint board meetings could be held in the OBC language or other arrangements could be made as necessary to facilitate communication. However, in most immigrant churches in the United States, the situation is typically analogous to the Jerusalem church in that OBCs have some level of bilingual language proficiency and many LBCs only know or are fluent in the language of the host culture. By

---

[69] Daily operations (Acts 2:45; 4:34-5:2; 15:36-41). Special issues that impact everyone (Acts 1:23; 6:2-3, 5-6; 11:22; 15:4, 12, 22).

[70] Acts 2:45; 4:34-5:2; 15:36-41.

[71] Capper, "Community of Goods," 353; Keener, *Acts 3:1–14:28*, K.l. 2:8582–8627; Marshall, *Acts*, 125–26; Witherington, *Acts*, 241.

minimizing joint board meetings through the use of separate boards for daily operations and only initiating joint boards to handle special issues that impact everyone, parallel ministry minimizes the language and cultural issues that alienate LBCs from the board.[72]

The separate and joint boards of the parallel ministry model most effectively address the problem of power struggles on the board. Typically, there is a power struggle and tension on the board over who will be the board chair, an OBC or LBC. There is also a power struggle involving the issue of the number of members from each congregation who will sit on the board. Ordinarily, the bilingual and separate service models attempt to address this concern by making board representation based on congregational size or by having equal numbers of board members regardless of congregational size. The church planting model addresses these issues through an independent LBC church that meets the needs of some LBCs, while leaving the needs of LBCs and OBCs in the immigrant church unmet. By implementing separate boards with equal authority, the parallel ministry model minimizes these tensions by moving them from routine frequently occurring board meetings to special infrequent joint board meetings.[73] Furthermore, since OBCs and LBCs both have a board chair and there are spiritual-relational understandings of equal authority (Acts 6:2-4, 6) and interdependence for the mutual meeting of needs (Acts 6:7), then parallel ministry's infrequent joint board meetings will be more amicable than bilingual or separate service meetings and more attractive to LBCs.

A final special concern regarding separate and joint boards is that of church discipline (Matt. 18:15-17; 2 Thess. 3:14-15). Since the culture of OBCs and LBCs is so different, then issues of church discipline are typically difficult to resolve. The difficulty lies both in the interpretation of Scripture and in the application of biblical principles. Frequently, OBCs and LBCs interpret the church discipline passages differently and often OBCs implement cultural practices for resolving problems rather than following biblical principles. Furthermore, unlike a church in a host culture, where incidents requiring church discipline are often a routine aspect of daily operations and do not impact the whole church, the situation is more complicated in an immigrant church and particularly a parallel ministry.

---

[72] Daily operations (Acts 2:45; 4:34-5:2; 15:36-41). Special issues that impact everyone (Acts 1:23; 6:2-3, 5-6; 11:22; 15:4, 12, 22).

[73] Acts 2:45; 4:34-5:2; 15:36-41.

In an immigrant church, church discipline is somewhat a daily operation and so should be handled by the separate boards regarding members of each respective congregation.[74] However, since frequently LBC members are the children of OBC members, then in some sense, church discipline impacts the whole church and so requires a joint board meeting.[75] Furthermore, it is possible that practical matters of church discipline will involve relationships or incidents between OBCs and LBCs. To resolve these two types of incidents, Acts 6:1-7 may be applied in the following manner.

In the first case, where an incident involves an OBC or LBC with another member of the same congregation, then the event should be considered a matter of daily operation and should be resolved by the respective OBC or LBC board.[76] If the OBC or LBC has relatives involved in the other respective congregation, then a joint board meeting should be called to report on the action taken. However, the joint board should not overrule the decision of the separate board. In the second case, if an incident requiring church discipline occurs between members of different congregations, then this event should be considered something that impacts the whole church and requires the joint board to resolve the issue.[77] It is not possible to cover how Acts 6:1-7 applies to every specific occurrence, and so the preceding applications are general. For example, an incident requiring church discipline may occur between two LBCs, but OBCs witnessed it. In this case, the best application is for the LBC board to decide the matter since LBCs are the ones needing discipline and the OBCs were only witnesses. Alternately, an OBC board member may embezzle church funds from the OBC account, but the LBCs contributed a large amount to the OBCs. In this case, the best application of Acts 6 may be for a joint OBC-LBC board to decide the matter because the indiscretion impacts the whole church. Parallel ministry churches will need to use wisdom in applying Acts 6:1-7 to cases of church discipline.

---

[74] Acts 2:45; 4:34-5:2; 15:36-41.

[75] Acts 1:23; 6:2-3, 5-6; 11:22; 15:4, 12, 22.

[76] Acts 2:45; 4:34-5:2; 15:36-41.

[77] Acts 1:23, 6:2-3, 5-6; 11:22; 15:4, 12, 22.

With regard to parallel budgets, in Acts 6 it is likely that the apostles transferred the financial and decision-making authority to the Hellenists for the widows' distribution for the whole church and not just the Hellenist widows, because there were widows in both groups.[78] However, in contemporary application, since OBCs and LBCs are in separate groups or typically there are no LBCs in the OBC ministry like there were widows in both groups in Acts 6, then when OBCs transfer financial and decision-making authority to LBCs, it is for the LBC ministry and not the whole church. Therefore, just as the seven Hellenists were a leadership team with full financial responsibility for their area of ministry (the widows' distribution, Acts 6:2) and the apostles/Hebraists for their area (prayer and the Word, Acts 6:2-4), so OBCs have a board and a budget for their ministry and LBCs have theirs. In a typical OBC church, the LBC ministry is one line-item on the church budget. While this situation may be acceptable for early stages of church growth when LBCs are exclusively or primarily a children's ministry and/or youth group, many OBC churches continue to maintain one line-item in the budget for LBC ministries that also have children, college students, young adults, and families.

If OBCs have only made plans for, but not taken some steps of actual implementation of parallel ministry, such as opening a separate bank account for LBCs by the time they are youth, then the OBCs are likely reluctant to transfer financial and decision-making authority. The

---

[78] Keener has the Hellenists in charge of the all the widows, while Capper and Marshall have the Hellenists in charge of the Hellenist widows only. Capper, "Community of Goods," 353–54; Keener, *Acts 3:1–14:28*, K.l. 2:9263–67; Marshall, *Acts*, 125. The fact that the phrases, "the community of disciples" (vs. 2), "brothers, you select" (vs. 3), "in the opinion of the whole community" (vs. 5), and "they placed before" (vs. 6), indicate that the whole congregation was involved favors Keener's interpretation that the Hellenists were put in charge of the widows in both groups. In favor of Capper and Marshall's interpretation that the Hellenists were put in charge of the widows only in the Hellenistic group is the use of the definite article and demonstrative pronoun "τῆς χρείας ταύτης" [*this* need] (Acts 6:3) to specify the particular need of the Hellenist widows in vs. 1. The decisive element in the passage seems to be that if the seven Hellenists only took care of the needs of the Hellenist widows, then the task of caring for the Hebraic widows would seem to fall back on the apostles. However, this possibility is eliminated by the claim that, by putting the seven in charge of the need, the apostles would be able to focus exclusively on "prayer and the ministry of the word" and not on meeting the needs of the widows (vs. 3–4). Therefore, the Hellenists must have been put in charge of the widows in both congregations so that the apostles would not have to deal with this responsibility and could focus exclusively on prayer and the ministry of the Word.

application of the transfer of financial authority (Acts 6:2) to the contemporary situation of OBCs and LBCs in parallel ministry is that both groups collect their own offering, put it in their own bank account, and use it for their own budgets, while interdependence means that they share resources with the whole church in order to meet everyone's needs (Acts 2:44-45, 6:7). If immigration from the home country stops or the OBC congregation ages, then the LBCs will need to contribute more to the declining OBC congregation. Just as OBCs voluntarily place funds in the LBC bank account when LBCs are young and financially dependent, LBCs should voluntarily place funds in the OBC bank account as the immigrant congregation ages or shrinks due to immigration patterns. Both the bylaws and the spiritual-relational aspect of the crisis may ensure that such interdependence occurs in imitation of the situation in Acts 6.

For a further depiction of what separate boards look like, see Figures 1 and 2 on the next two pages.

Figure 1: Typical Immigrant Church Organizational Structure

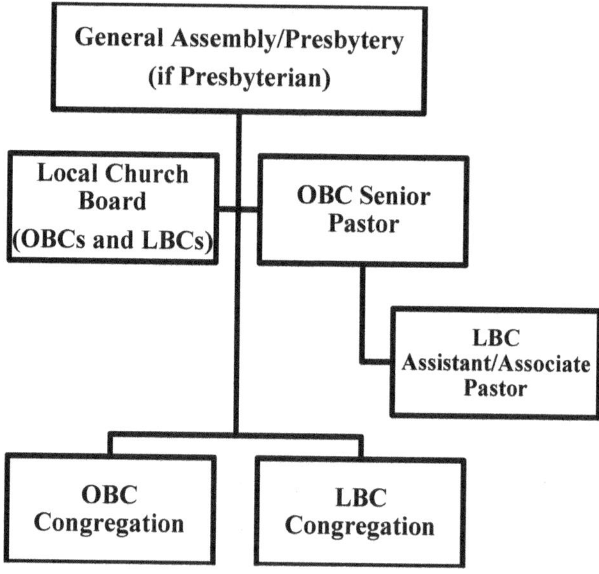

Note that in this model pastoral reporting is from the Assistant/Associate to the Senior and from the Senior to the board. In this model, there is much tension in the OBC-LBC pastor relationship and communication between the LBC pastor and the board is minimized and difficult.

Figure 2: Parallel Ministry Organizational Structure

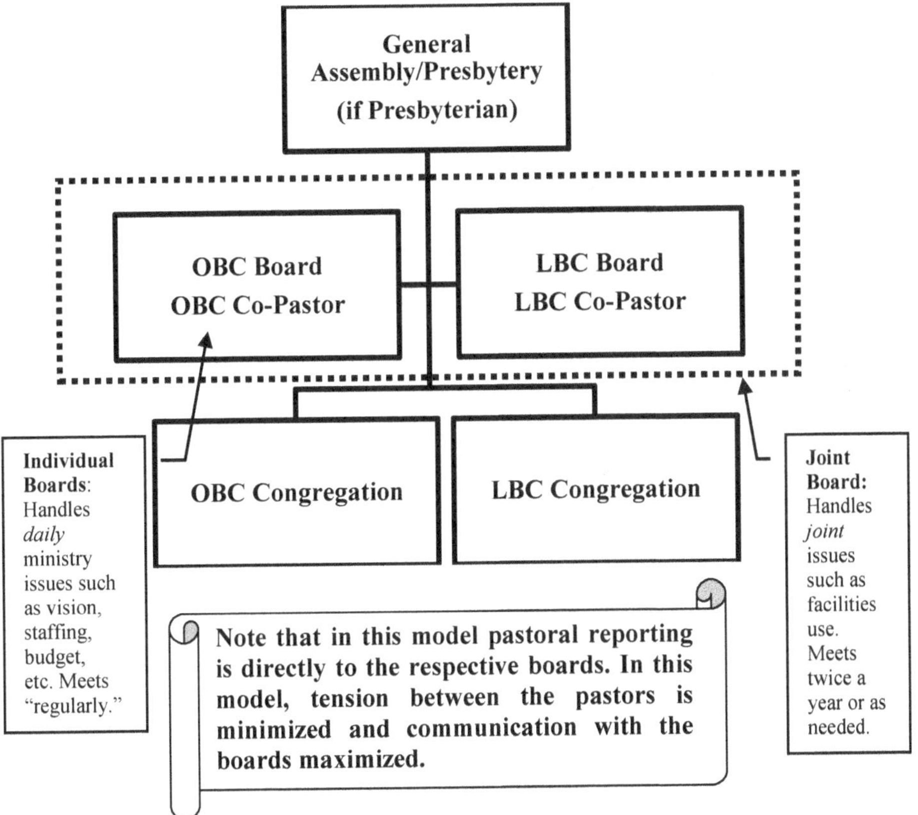

Therefore, according to Acts 6:1-7, parallel ministry entails interdependent (Acts 6:7) and culturally relevant ministries to OBCs and LBCs (Acts 6:1), each with their own financial (Acts 6:2) and decision-making authority (Acts 6:3-6). Parallel ministry also involves separate OBC and LBC boards, budgets, co-pastors, services, and so on. These features of parallel ministry better meet the concerns and needs of both OBCs and LBCs than the alternatives. However, many readers likely have at least some questions or objections in mind with regard to the presentation of parallel ministry in this chapter. In the next chapter, the proposal for parallel ministry in this chapter is summarized and responses are given to some common objections to parallel ministry.

CHAPTER 3: Current Proposal

One Sunday as I was leaving the sanctuary after a particularly grueling Easter joint service, I was stopped outside by one of the church elders. Even after years of serving at the church, it was the first time he had taken the initiative to talk to me. I do not remember the exact details of the conversation on that sunny Southern California day more than a decade ago, but I remember the warmth of the sun on my skin and a gentle sea breeze coming in off the ocean. The conversation went something like this:

"Doesn't seem like many of the English group made it today," the elder said to me.

Surprised by his directness, I replied sheepishly with my eyes cast down like a kid with his hand caught in the cookie jar, "No, it doesn't seem like many of them made it." I braced myself for his response. I knew that at least half of the English congregation regularly skipped the joint services. In fact, just last week one of the English leaders and his wife had told me that they had been sharing their faith with another couple whom they wanted to bring to church, particularly on one of the days that churches traditionally stress preaching the Gospel, such as Easter or Christmas. However, they wanted the new couple to hear the Gospel in their own language—English. So they explained to me that they would not be in the joint Easter service.

The elder then sighed wistfully and with evident pain said, "It has been years since my children attended our church." He paused.

I was greatly relieved by his response and at the same time deeply moved by his pain. This was the first time an OBC had ever openly shared with me their understanding of the silent exodus and their personal grief over its impact on their lives. I didn't know what to say. It didn't matter. Talking to older OBCs is like talking to your parents as a kid, *they* asked the questions, *they* expressed their opinions, you listened, and when *they* were done talking, the conversation was over.

With an energy and frankness that are rarely seen in older reserved Asian men, he exuded forcefully, "We should have given the English group more freedom. Those old men on the board are set in their ways."

I tried to maintain a poker face. I found this both hilarious and shocking; shocking because I never knew he felt that way, and because he had to save face by not directly disagreeing, he had never given any indication in the board meetings of his feelings. I found it hilarious because, ironically, he was one of the old men he was deriding.

He went on, "If I was in charge, I would do things differently." He sighed again, choked up at bit, and said softly, "It's too late for my family." I was again deeply moved by his openness and sadness.

Regaining his composure, he looked around slowly at the other younger families. As he left, he patted me on the shoulder with a fatherly tenderness and whispered just loud enough for me to hear, "But I am still on the board." I took that to indicate that there was still hope for the other families.

This OBC elder was not quite right in his solution, but he was on the right track—the LBCs needed interdependence.

In the last chapter, from a detailed exegesis of Acts 6:1-7, the basic outline of parallel ministry and some supplemental points were drawn, both of which contributed to a normative definition of parallel ministry. Additionally, some of the points received further clarification. In this chapter, the conclusions of the exegesis from chapter 2 are summarized and an argument is made for the normative nature of those conclusions. The method of the current proposal is also contrasted with that of the three past proposals. Finally, some responses are given to some of the common objections to parallel ministry.

Proposal Summary

In chapter 2, a detailed exegesis of Acts 6:1-7 yielded the basic outline of parallel ministry and some supplemental points, from which a normative definition was developed. The exegesis focused on Acts 6:1-7 as the definitive passage for dealing with the crisis of the immigrant church, because it resolves a cultural conflict similar to the one between contemporary OBCs and LBCs with explicit principles and implied details that not only define the parallel ministry model, but also exclude the bilingual, separate service, and church planting models.

In the familiar passage of Acts 6:1-7, the account is given of a cultural dispute within the early church whereby the Hellenistic Jewish Christians charged the Hebraic Jewish Christians with not meeting the needs of Hellenist widows in the distribution of daily support. The dispute was resolved by the whole church's acceptance of the apostles' proposal to delegate the task of distributing support to leaders that the community selected and they commissioned. Seven Hellenistic leaders, including Stephen and Philip, were assigned the task of meeting the widows' needs. As a result, the church continued to grow by reaching unbelievers. The passage indicates that cultural conflicts between groups similar to OBCs and LBCs are resolved by transferring financial and decision-making power to the LBCs so that they may have a culturally relevant ministry that meets their needs and has the capacity to reach the lost.

The exegesis of Acts 6:1-7 consisted of two main parts. First, six points were drawn from the text that are explicitly present in the meaning of Acts 6:1-7. These points formed the basic outline or definition of parallel ministry. Second, five additional points were drawn from the text, which are implications of the meaning and are supplemental to the basic definition of parallel ministry.

The following six points form the basic outline of parallel ministry and are drawn from the textual details and explicit meaning of the narrative in Acts 6:1-7:

1. *Valid Analogy*: In Acts 6:1, the conflict between the Hebraic and Hellenistic Jewish Christians presents a "valid analogy" or an example that can be accurately compared to the cultural situation of OBCs and LBCs in the contemporary immigrant church.
2. *Unmet Needs*: Just as the Hellenistic Jews were complaining that the Hebraic Jews were not meeting their needs (Acts 6:1), the contemporary immigrant church OBCs are not meeting the needs of LBCs.

3. *Transfer of Financial Authority*: In Acts 6:2, as their response to the complaint, the apostles (OBCs) resolved the conflict by transferring financial authority from themselves (Acts 4:34-37; 5:2)/the Hebraists (Acts 6:1-2) to the Hellenistic Jews (LBCs, Acts 6:5).
4. *Transfer of Decision-Making Authority*: In Acts 6:3 and 5-6, as their response to the complaint, the apostles (OBCs) resolved the conflict by transferring decision-making authority for meeting the needs of the Hellenists (LBCs) to the Hellenists (LBCs).
5. *One Church Interdependence*: Even though there was a transfer of financial and decision-making authority, the church still functioned as one church, the Jerusalem Church, with interdependence between the Hebraic (OBCs) and Hellenistic (LBCs) Jewish Christians (Acts 6:7).
6. *Unbelievers Reached*: In Acts 6:7, as a result of the resolution of the conflict, the church was able to reach unbelievers from both groups.

The following five additional points include elements that are supplemental to the basic outline of parallel ministry and/or are only implied by Acts 6:1-7:

1. *Parallel Meetings*: In Acts 6:1, the Hebraists (OBCs) and Hellenists (LBCs) were likely meeting in separate houses for worship as evidenced by significant biblical and extra-biblical evidences (archeological and manuscript evidence).
2. *Control over Staffing*: In Acts 6:2-6, while the apostles/Hebraists (OBCs) took the initiative to resolve the problem so that the Hellenist's needs would be met, the whole church participated in the solution so that the Hellenists (LBCs) retained control over their staffing and leadership.
3. *Spiritual-Relational Aspect*: In Acts 6:2 and 5, both the Hebraists (OBCs) and Hellenists (LBCs) displayed spiritual-relational dispositions or attitudes that allowed for the solution (Acts 6:1-6).
4. *Different Visions*: The Hebraists (OBCs) and Hellenists (LBCs) remained one church as they successfully

reached the lost of both groups, while pursuing different visions (Acts 6:1, 7).

5. *Equal Authority*: The Hebraic (OBC) and Hellenistic (LBC) Jewish Christian leaders had equal authority after the disciple's solution was implemented (Acts 6:2-4, 6).

(For an example of what parallel ministry looks like, see Table 1 in the list of tables.)

While proponents of the separate service model do not provide a consistent definition of parallel ministry (see chapter 5), the preceding eleven points drawn from the exegesis of Acts 6 allow for a uniform and authoritative definition of parallel ministry.

While the main structural components and supplemental points provide a broad outline for parallel ministry, it is possible to make some more specific contemporary applications to the contemporary immigrant church. The application of these main structural components and supplemental points to the contemporary immigrant church results in:

1. Co-pastors rather than a hierarchy (often expressed as team leadership).
2. Parallel services.
3. Parallel boards.
4. Parallel budgets.
5. Separate visions.
6. Interdependence in terms of OBC children attending the LBC children's ministry, Sunday school, youth group, and other fellowships.
7. Interdependence in the form of OBCs financially supporting LBCs early in ministry and LBCs supporting OBCs later in ministry.
8. Interdependence through some joint culturally relevant activities not including joint services.

If it is not clear how some of the eleven points are drawn from Acts 6:1-7 or how some of the specific applications follow from the list of eleven points regarding parallel ministry and why they are significant to immigrant church ministry, then the detailed explanations in chapter 2 may provide some clarification. (Also see Figures 1 and 2 in the list of illustrations.)

According to Acts 6:1-7, the ecclesiastical parallel ministry structure exists when favorable spiritual-relational conditions occur in such a way that OBCs transfer financial and decision-making authority to LBCs so that they may create a culturally relevant and interdependent ministry that allows for the needs of both groups to be met. In this interpretation of Acts 6:1-7, the passage explicitly and implicitly states that the parallel ministry ecclesiastical structure consists, not only of separate and culturally relevant OBC and LBC worship services, but also co-pastors and different offerings, budgets, boards, and visions that are part of a single interdependent church. The various elements that make up the structure are "parallel" because, while OBCs and LBCs each have their separate respective ecclesiastical components, those components are interdependent rather than independent or dependent upon each other. To gain a further understanding of the parallel ministry structure, please see Figures 1 and 2 and Tables 1 and 3 in the lists of illustrations and tables.

The alternatives to parallel ministry include bilingual worship, separate worship services, and church planting. Bilingual worship involves using some type of translation between the OBC and LBC languages, typically only in a worship service. Separate services involve different worship services for OBCs and LBCs that meet at different times and/or locations. Church planting seeks to plant LBC churches that are independent from OBC churches. Parallel ministry is superior to these alternatives, not only because alternative methods have a deficient biblical basis to parallel ministry's firm foundation in Acts 6:1-7 and because they fail to adequately deal with the concerns and needs presented in chapter 1, but also because these alternatives do not provide a normative solution to the crisis.

Unique and Normative Nature

The construction of the parallel ministry model differs methodologically from the other ecclesiastical models both in its use of sociology and Scripture and in its normative nature. The parallel ministry model uses sociology to describe the problem, but uses the Bible to provide the solution. In the other models, sociology not only describes the problem, but ultimately provides the solution. For examples, see the analysis of the alternative solutions in chapter 5.[1]

In contrast to the other models which allow for sociological factors to determine church structure, the parallel ministry model takes Acts 6:1-7 to be universally normative, because the passage is intended as a moral example to be imitated and because the subject matter of the narrative matches the practical crisis to be resolved. Acts 6:1-7 is normative, not only because it is part of God's authoritative Word (2 Tim. 3:16-17), but also because there is general agreement that Luke wrote his history rhetorically to make specific points through his individual narratives and the overall story of the book as a whole.[2] Some of the narratives serve as theological examples and others as ethical examples.[3]

---

[1] For the sociological and other problems associated with alternative solutions see: *Ethnic Chinese Congress on World Evangelization* [ECCWE]. Fred Cheung, "Bridging Racial and Linguistic Gaps," in *ECCWE*, ed. Sharon Wai–Man Chan (Tsim Sha Tsui, Hong Kong: Chinese Coordination Centre of World Evangelism, 1986), 67–68; William L. Eng, "Having an Effective Model for ABC Ministry within the Chinese Church," in *FACE* (Oakland, CA: Fellowship of American Chinese Evangelicals (FACE), 2009), 110, 119; Ken Uyeda Fong, *Pursuing the Pearl: A Comprehensive Resource for Multi–Asian Ministry*, Updated ed. (Valley Forge, PA: Judson Press, 1999), 5–6, 25, 194, 218; Russell Jeung, *Faithful Generations: Race and New Asian American Churches*, Kindle ed. (New Brunswick, NJ: Rutgers University Press, 2005), K.l. 1595–2509; Samuel Ling and Clarence Cheuk, *The "Chinese" Way of Doing Things: Perspectives on American–Born Chinese and the Chinese Church in North America* (Phillipsburg, NJ: P & R Publishing, 1999), 169, 206–07; Manuel Ortiz, *The Hispanic Challenge: Opportunities Confronting the Church* (Downers Grove: InterVarsity, 1993), 123, 117–25, 143–77; Mercidieu Phillips, "Resolving the Causes of Second Generation Exodus from the Haitian Church in South Florida" (D.Ed.Min. diss., Bethel Seminary, Saint Paul, MN, 2011), 31–32, 105, 158–59; Peter Tow, "How to Solve the Linguistic Problem in the North American Chinese Church," in *ECCWE*, ed. Sharon Wai–Man Chan (Tsim Sha Tsui, Hong Kong: Chinese Coordination Centre of World Evangelism, 1986), 116; Joseph C. Wong, "The Biblical Basis for Promoting Effective ABC Ministries," in *FACE* (Oakland, CA: FACE, 2009), 119–20; Wayland Wong, "Who Are the American–Born Chinese?," in *FACE* (Oakland, CA: FACE, 2009), 28–31, 47; David K. Woo, "Introduction," in *FACE* (Oakland, CA: FACE, 2009), 161–62.

[2] Darrell L. Bock, *Acts*, BECNT (Grand Rapids: Baker Academic, 2007), in *Logos Library System* [CD–ROM], 11; Dean E. Flemming, *Contextualization in the New Testament: Patterns for Theology and Mission* (Downers Grove: InterVarsity Press, 2005), 26–27; Mikeal C. Parsons, *Acts*, PCNT (Grand Rapids: Baker Academic, 2008), in *Logos Library System* [CD–ROM], 4, 7–10; David G. Peterson, *The Acts of the*

For instance, Acts 15 (the Jerusalem Council) is a theological example that deals with salvation by grace through faith apart from works, but Acts 5:1–11 (the death of Ananias and Sapphira) is a moral example that teaches honesty. The ethical examples may be positive paradigms to imitate or negative patterns to avoid. Although there is some disagreement as to the universal applicability of some of the theological examples, such as those involving speaking in tongues and baptism of the Spirit, there seems to be general agreement that the ethical examples of the Bible generally and Acts specifically are normative or binding.[4]

For example, not only do scholars in biblical studies argue that Luke's intention in Acts is rhetorical, but also ethicists claim that Scripture teaches some sort of virtue or character ethic in which the Bible teaches us what kind of people we ought to be by providing positive and negative moral examples through narratives that are to be imitated and avoided.[5] Acts 6:1-7 is an ethical example by definition, because it deals with the moral issue of resolving cultural conflict between two cultural-linguistic groups.[6] As a positive ethical example of how to resolve such cultural conflicts through ecclesiology (the structure of church government), Acts 6 is a normative example to be universally imitated.

Although the size, resources, and other practical circumstantial factors of a congregation will impact a church's ability to implement the parallel ministry solution in Acts 6, none of these factors change the biblical goal toward which the church should be working, namely parallel

---

Apostles, PNTC (Grand Rapids: W.B. Eerdmans, 2009), in *Logos Library System* [CD–ROM], 21–22; Timothy Wiarda, "The Jerusalem Council and the Theological Task," *JETS* 46, no. 2 (2003): 244; Ben Witherington, III, *The Acts of the Apostles: A Socio–Rhetorical Commentary* (Grand Rapids: W. B. Eerdmans, 1998), in *Logos Library System* [CD–ROM], 43.

[3] For a similar judgment see: Wiarda, "Theological Task," 244–45.

[4] Wayne A. Grudem, "Preface," in *Are Miraculous Gifts for Today?: Four Views*, Kindle ed., Wayne A. Grudem, ed., Counterpoints (Grand Rapids: Zondervan, 2011), K.l. 54–105.

[5] D. Michael Cox and Brad J. Kallenberg, "Character," in *DSE*, Kindle ed., Joel B. Green, ed. (Grand Rapids: Baker Academic, 2011), 5841–5844; Nikki Coffey Tousley and Brad J. Kallenberg, "Virtue Ethics," in *DSE*, Kindle ed., Joel B. Green, ed. (Grand Rapids: Baker Academic, 2011), 32628–32629, 32643–32646. On the Bible's teaching of imitation of moral exemplars see: 2 Kgs 14:3; Eccl 9:13; John 13:34–35; 1 Cor 4:16; 10:6, 11; 11:1; Gal 4:12; Phil 3:17; 4:9; 1 Thess 1:6; 2:14; Heb 6:12, 13:7; 1 Pet 2:21).

[6] For a similar judgment see: Parsons, *Acts*, 82.

ministry.[7] The argument that size, resources, or other practical factors changes the goal of parallel ministry (Acts 6:1–7) is akin to the argument that since people lack the resources to avoid lying, then truth telling should no longer be the goal (Col. 3:9). People may fail to live up to biblical standards due to a lack of knowledge (Lev. 4:27–28; Luke 12:48) or power (Rom. 5:6; 7:18–20; 8:3), but such failure does not change the moral standard.

Furthermore, Acts 6:1-7 is normative because the subject matter of the narrative matches the practical crisis to be resolved. One of the problems with some of the other ministry models, such as Pai's bilingual model and Fong's appeal to Act 15, is that they draw on biblical passages which do not have the same subject matter as the crisis to be resolved and therefore do not establish good analogies. For a biblical principle or narrative example to apply to a contemporary situation, there should be some sort of connection between the two by means of similarity or a valid analogy must exist. In order for an analogy to be valid, the "Analogies do not require that the example used as an analogy be *just* like the example in the conclusion," but "Analogies require only *relevant* similarities."[8] In the case of Acts 6:1-7, the subject matter of resolving cultural conflict between two groups by means of leadership restructuring (ecclesiology or the structure of church government) is very similar to the contemporary crisis of the immigrant church. Since Acts 6:1-7 contains such a strong analogy to the crisis of the immigrant church and since this seems to be the only such biblical example specifically dealing with a similar issue, then it seems not only to be normative, but also to take precedence over lesser analogies that may be drawn from Scripture.

Objections and Responses

This section provides responses to some of the common objections to parallel ministry. The objections and responses to the separate service model (chapter 5) generally apply to the parallel ministry model, since the separate service is really a partial parallel ministry.

[7] Eng, "Effective Model," 119.

[8] Emphasis original. Anthony Weston, *A Rulebook for Arguments*, 2nd ed. (Indianapolis: Hackett Publishing Company, 1992), 25–26.

However, there are some further objections to the parallel ministry model which reveal some of its strengths and weaknesses.

No different from church planting. One of the most likely objections to the parallel ministry model is that it is no different from a church plant since both models have separate leadership, boards, budgets, visions, church names, and so on. However, the main difference between the two models is that while church plants create an *independent* church, parallel ministry creates two *interdependent* congregations that are one church.

Since it is important for OBCs not to divide their families, then it is significant that the Bible defines the parallel ministry solution as "one church" (Acts 6:7). In parallel ministry, physical unity is compromised (John 4:19–24), but spiritual unity (Eph. 4:2–3) is maintained by preserving one church (Acts 6:7). The parallel ministry model envisions an LBC congregation that either shares a facility with an OBC congregation or is very close geographically, such as right next door, just like in the separate service model.[9] The geographic closeness allows for the children of OBCs to attend the LBC congregation so that the needs of both OBCs and all LBCs are met (Acts 6:1), unlike in the church planting model, where typically only the needs of LBCs who are unchurched or part of the exodus are met. Furthermore, while the congregations will not have joint services, they may have some joint activities, board meetings, pastoral visitation, and/or bylaws.

OBCs historically have never agreed. Another likely objection to the parallel ministry model is that OBCs historically have never agreed to it, so there is no reason to believe that they will agree to it now and that is why LBC church plants have formed.[10] This objection is contrary to the faith, hope, and love that believers are to exhibit in the Spirit (1 Cor. 13:13) and by which they are to carry out Christian ministry in the church (1 Thess. 1:3). In the past, one reason that others have written on the crisis of the immigrant church is that they have hope that the crisis may be resolved and the situation improved by continued

---

[9] Phillips, "Haitian Church," 135.

[10] Fong, *Multi–Asian Ministry*, 185, 194, 197, 223; Jeung, *Faithful Generations*, K.l.2232–33; Jonathan Tran, "Why Asian American Christianity Has No Future: The over against, Leaving Behind, and Separation from of Asian American Christian Identity," *SANACS*, no. 2 (Sum 2010): 25, 28.

dialogue.[11] This proposal contributes to that dialogue by providing a more solid biblical basis for a solution to the crisis in the hope that OBCs in faith will recognize the normative nature of Acts 6 and will move toward parallel ministry because of love of God and their LBC children.

There is hope also as there are cases in which some churches have approximated parallel ministry more recently.[12] As mentioned in the evaluation of the church planting model (chapter 5), if OBCs will not take the initiative to create parallel ministries from within the OBC church, then perhaps LBCs can plant churches outside with the intent of partnering with an existing OBC church to create a parallel ministry as some have unintentionally done and thereby approximated a parallel ministry.[13] However, both the participation of OBCs in independent LBC churches and the partnering of independent LBC churches with immigrant churches indicate the desperate need for parallel ministry to meet the needs of both OBCs and LBCs.

Acts 6 is not a valid analogy. Someone might object that Acts 6 is not a valid analogy because Hebraic Jews are not similar to OBCs and Hellenistic Jews are not similar to LBCs. The objection may run as follows: In an immigration situation, there are at least three groups of people: the host culture, the immigrants, and the immigrant's children. In Acts 6, since the Hellenists have immigrated to Jerusalem, then they are like OBCs who come from their homeland to a foreign place and the Hellenist's children are like the LBCs. The Hebraists, who live in Jerusalem, are like the host culture of the land to which the Hellenists have immigrated. This objection, however, misclassifies the three groups by

---

[11] Ortiz, *Hispanic Challenge*, 19; Phillips, "Haitian Church," 15; Daniel A. Rodriguez, *A Future for the Latino Church: Models for Multilingual, Multigenerational Hispanic Congregations*, Kindle ed. (IVP Academic, 2011), K.l. 78–79; Woo, "Introduction," 6.

[12] William L. Eng, "An Overview of Christian Work among ABCs," in *FACE* (Oakland, CA: FACE, 2009), 57–63; Phillips, "Haitian Church," 135; Rodriguez, *Latino Church*, K.l. 544–752; Kathleen Sullivan, "Catherine's Catholic Church: One Church, Parallel Congregations," in *Religion and the New Immigrants: Continuities and Adaptations*, Kindle ed., Helen Rose Ebaugh and Janet Saltzman Chafetz, eds.(Walnut Creek, CA: Altamira Press, 2000), pp. 255–90.

[13] Fong, *Multi–Asian Ministry*, 193; Jeung, *Faithful Generations*, K.l. 1115–16; Rodriguez, *Latino Church*, K.l. 986–87.

focusing on geographic rather than historic, ethnic, cultural, and language considerations.

Historically, the host or dominant culture was the Roman Empire or Greco-Roman culture of which Jerusalem and the Jewish people were a part. Ethnically, the Hebraic and Hellenistic Jews were the same as each other and different from the host culture, like contemporary OBCs and LBCs. Culturally and linguistically, the Hebraic and Hellenistic Jews differed from each other much like OBCs and LBCs. The Hellenists are like LBCs in that they speak the language of the host culture and have assimilated to the host culture, while the Hebraists are like OBCs in that they speak a language different from the host culture and have not assimilated. Furthermore, the Hebraic Jews are like OBCs in that they are the ones in control of the financial and decision-making authority in the church, and the Hellenistic Jews are like LBCs in being under their authority. It is true that, geographically, the Hebraic Jews were living in their homeland and the Hellenistic Jews were returning to their homeland so that there are some differences between the Hebraic and Hellenistic Jews and OBCs and LBCs. However, the historic, ethnic, cultural, and language similarities seem to be more important and to outweigh the geographic dissimilarities so that a valid analogy exists between the various groups. Analogies are never exact comparisons and neither is the one between Acts 6 and OBCs and LBCs. Valid analogies merely need to make reasonably similar comparisons, and the historic, ethnic, cultural, and language similarities between Acts 6 and OBCs and LBCs are similar enough so as to establish a valid comparison.

Acts 6 does not exclude creative adaptation. Some may object that, although Acts 6:1-7 may be normative in some sense, its authority as an example does not demand that the paradigm in the text be mindlessly mimicked or copied exactly, but rather that the narrative exemplifies principles that may be creatively adapted to various circumstances.[14]

---

[14] At least two commentators may give the impression that Acts 6 might be adapted freely. Ricahrd N. Longenecker, *The Acts of the Apostles*, ed. Frank E. Gaebelein and J. D. Douglas, in vol. 9 of *EBC* (Grand Rapids: Zondervan, Regency Reference Library, 1981), in *QuickVerse* [CD–ROM], (Grand Rapids, MI: The Zondervan Corporation, 1976), 331; Peterson, *Acts*, 233. In ethics there has been much scholarly debate over the nature of imitation. There is a consensus at least among some that imitation involves cognitive repetition rather than mindless mimicry. Jo–Ann Brant, "The Place of Mimēsis in Paul's Thought," *Studies in Religion/Sciences religieuses* 22, no. 3 (1993): 287; Jason G. Weaver, "Paul's Call to Imitation: The Rhetorical Function of the Theme of Imitation in Its Epistolary Context" (Ph.D. diss., The Catholic University of America, Washington, D.C., 2013), 10–45.

However, if the other three models are considered creative adaptations of Acts 6:1-7, they are all inadequate because they ignore some of the principles or features in the biblical text. The bilingual model does not allow for a transfer of financial and decision-making authority. The separate service model does not allow for staffing control or a culturally relevant vision. The church planting model does not allow for interdependence. All of these inadequacies historically have resulted in a failure of each model to meet the needs of LBCs as occurred in Acts 6:1. The only available model that faithfully implements Acts 6 in such a way as to meet the needs of both OBCs and LBCs successfully is the parallel ministry model.As will be discussed in chapter 5, proponents of the church planting model claim that a weakness of parallel ministry is that it cannot reach highly assimilated LBCs, because they do not like the cultural atmosphere created by OBCs.[15] Not only does such an objection ignore the normative nature of Acts 6 as the solution to the crisis of the immigrant church, but it also runs counter to the historical evidence in which ministries that have approximated parallel ministry have been successful in creating culturally relevant ministries that have attracted LBCs of all generations.[16] If partial parallel ministries have historically had some success in reaching all kinds of LBCs and if full parallel ministries are biblically sound (Acts 6), then one would expect that true parallel ministries would be even more successful in meeting the needs of LBCs.

Acts 6 indicates one not multiple boards. Someone might object that since some verses in the account of the choosing of the seven (Acts 6:2, 3, 5) and the Jerusalem Council (Acts 15:4, 12, 22) may indicate that the whole church was involved, then the Jerusalem church (Acts 6:7) created or had one joint board. In response, although Acts 6 and Acts 15 are normative for church practice, special issues in both incidents are being discussed that involved the whole community. In Acts 6, cultural conflict (Acts 6:1) and, in Acts 15, the basis of salvation (Acts 15:1, 11) and table fellowship (Acts 15:20) threatened to destroy the unity of the

---

[15] Fong, *Multi–Asian Ministry*, 8–10, 25, 194, 218–19; Wong, "Future Need," 172–73; Tran, "Asian American No Future," 28.

[16] Jeung, *Faithful Generations*, K.l. 576, 579–80; Phillips, "Haitian Church," 13; Jonathan Tran, "Why Asian American Christianity is the Future: Holding It Together in Yellow Christianity," *SANACS*, no. 2 (Sum 2010): 45.

entire church. Since issues were being discussed that impacted the whole church, then it was necessary for the whole church to address them. However, when more routine issues were decided, as in the distribution of aid to the needy that did not involve cultural conflict (Acts 4:32-5:11), then individual leaders or smaller groups made the decisions. In fact, the main thrust of the solution in Acts 6 was to allow the Hellenists to make decisions about aid for widows apart from the Hebraic Jews (Acts 6:2-6). Therefore, if Acts 6 and 15 imply anything about a joint board for churches with different cultural-linguistic groups like OBCs and LBCs, then the implication is that joint boards are only necessary for special issues that impact the whole church (Acts 6:1; 15:1, 11), such as facilities decisions, and not daily operations, which may be decided by each group's leaders or boards respectively (Acts 6:2-6).

Some communities have LBCs but no OBCs. Proponents of the church planting model will surely refer to their demographic studies and object that some LBCs are in communities with no OBCs and are geographically too far from OBC churches to partner with them.[17] In response, the parallel ministry solution of Acts 6:1-7 is meant explicitly for churches that are experiencing cultural conflicts between OBCs and LBCs (Acts 6:1). If a community exists with no OBCs or LBCs live too far from an OBC church, then parallel ministry is not necessary, but LBC churches may still seek to find even distant OBC churches and find ways to help them develop parallel ministries. If OBCs allow for effective parallel LBC ministries, then in most cases LBC churches would be unnecessary. In general and in the current situation in which OBC churches have not chosen to develop parallel LBC ministries, LBC churches are really a detriment to OBC churches and the LBCs to whom they minister and the LBCs in those LBC churches. If the situation were different, then some LBCs might choose to plant independent LBC churches for strategic evangelistic or other reasons—other than the failure of OBC churches to effectively minister to them. However, in the current situation of the failure of OBC ministry to effectively reach LBCs, LBC churches (as wonderful as they may be in many ways) are ultimately counterproductive for both OBCs and LBCs.

Separate boards/visions are divisive. Someone might object that separate boards and visions will divide the church so that interdependence collapses and the two congregations become two

---

[17] David K. Woo, "Planting ABC Churches," in *FACE* (Oakland, CA: FACE, 2009), 162–64.

independent churches, particularly as the LBC ministry grows and becomes multicultural.[18] This is a possibility. However, several factors may mitigate the situation. First and most importantly, if parallel ministry from Acts 6 is taught to the congregation periodically from the pulpit, in the Sunday school, small groups, and/or other appropriate venues, then the church will have a biblical understanding to help keep the congregations together. Second, if the LBC parallel ministry is implemented early enough in the OBC church's lifecycle, then it is likely that at least some of the leaders in the LBC congregation will be the children of the OBC congregation's members. Their interests in their parents and grandparents will help keep the church together. Third, the church structure may be written into the bylaws. Fourth, if immigration stops, the OBC congregation will eventually disappear, and if the LBC congregation still exists at this time, then it will become independent.

Acts 6 indicates that OBCs retained control. Someone might object that, just as the apostles were Hebraic Jews who had authority over the whole church and the Hellenistic Jews were only given authority over a part of the church ministry under the authority of the apostles, OBCs are to maintain authority over the whole church through one board.[19] In response, it is important to consider at least four factors when applying Acts 6:1-7 to the contemporary setting of OBCs and LBCs. First, except for some branches of Pentecostals and Charismatics, most evangelicals consider that the office of an apostle ceased with the early church and that there is no equivalent office today. Second, since the Hebraic and Hellenistic Jews likely met separately in their own house churches, then they probably had their own elders or leaders, and the seven chosen in Acts 6 are more likely to be the Hellenistic leaders rather than merely deacons.[20] Third, in the contemporary situation, if there are no apostles,

---

[18] Rodriguez, *Latino Church*, K.l. 587–91, 848–50.

[19] Craig S. Keener, *Acts: An Exegetical Commentary*, Kindle ed., vol. 2 (Grand Rapids: Baker Academic, 2013), K.l. 9265–67; I. Howard Marshall, *The Acts of the Apostles: An Introduction and Commentary*, Reprint ed., TNTC, vol. 5 (Grand Rapids: William B. Eerdmans, 1989), 125.

[20] F. F. Bruce, *The Book of Acts*, Revised ed., NICNT (Grand Rapids: William B. Eerdmans, 1988), 121; Marshall, *Acts*, 125. There is great debate concerning whether or not the seven (Acts 6:5) are deacons or some other sort of leader. Readers may consult the commentaries on Acts cited throughout this work and in the bibliography

then the best extrapolation of Acts 6:1-7 is for OBCs and LBCs to have their own leaders (boards) like Hebraic and Hellenistic house churches had. Fourth, and as demonstrated in chapter 2, the language used in Acts 6:2-4 indicates that the Hellenistic leaders had equal authority to the Hebraic leaders after the financial and decision-making authority was transferred.[21]

The spectrum of assimilation allows for multiple applications. Church planting proponents may make another objection based on the sociological concept of the spectrum of assimilation or the idea that people are at different levels of assimilation along a scale. They may argue that just as Acts 6 allows for parallel ministry between OBCs and LBCs in a local church, so parallel ministries may be established between other groups and in different types of ministry settings. For example, they may claim that 1.5 and second generation LBCs may have parallel ministries. Likewise, they may apply the concept to establish parallel ministries between third, fourth, fifth, and so on generation LBCs. Similarly, they may claim that the parallel is not between dual congregations in one church, but rather between local churches and the universal church as one church. In response, the analogy between Acts 6 and parallel ministry for different groups of LBCs with various levels of assimilation is not a good parallel (not a valid analogy), because Acts 6 has different cultural-language groups of the same ethnicity, while LBCs typically are only separated by culture and not language or ethnicity. Furthermore, the appendix, A Postscript on Multicultural Churches, demonstrates that the situation in Acts 13:1 and not Acts 6 is applicable to the circumstance of LBCs with different levels of assimilation. Additionally, Fong's assumption that LBCs with different levels of assimilation are so different that they cannot exist in the same ministry has been shown to be mistaken by historical examples (chapter 5).

Parallel ministry is not necessary. Some existing churches with a bilingual or separate service model may object that parallel ministry

---

for a discussion of this issue. However, the commentaries reflect that the current scholarly consensus is that the seven were not deacons.

[21] Darin Hawkins Land, *The Diffusion of Ecclesiastical Authority: Sociological Dimensions of Leadership in the Book of Acts*, Princeton Theological Monograph Series, vol. 90, Kindel ed. (Eugene, OR: Pickwick, 2008), K.l. 3683–84, 3687–88; Parsons, *Acts*, 84; Peterson, *Acts*, 235. Capper makes a different argument, but its result is a stitution where both groups have equal authority. Brian Capper, "The Palestinian Cultural Context of Earliest Christian Community of Goods," in *BAPS*, 353–54.

is not necessary because their LBCs are happy and their church is healthy. While some immigrant churches without parallel ministry may appear to be healthy to various members from either generation or congregation, this appearance is a false one generated by the illusion of success.22 Acts 6 is the biblical solution to the crisis of the immigrant church, and if a church is not following this solution, time will reveal that there is a problem. However, by the time the church realizes it is in trouble, it may already be too late. It is far better for the health of immigrant churches to submit to God's plan for parallel ministry in Acts 6 from the outset.

Parallel ministry is segregation. In the same way that some object that the homogeneous unit principle amounts to segregation, some may object that dividing a single heterogeneous OBC-LBC congregation into two homogeneous OBC and LBC parallel congregations is segregation.23 In response, the basis, motive, and means of parallel ministry are completely different between segregation and the homogeneous unit. Whereas the homogenous unit is a sociological principle, parallel ministry is biblically based on Acts 6:1-7. Whereas segregation is intended to oppress, parallel ministry is intended to meet needs. Whereas segregation is imposed externally by force, parallel ministry is implemented internally by voluntary request. Furthermore, whereas OBCs typically want to maintain a homogenous unit in their church by reaching out only to OBCs and discouraging LBCs from reaching out to groups other than LBCs of the same ethnicity, parallel ministry allows LBCs, if they so choose, to create a heterogeneous congregation of LBCs, people from the host culture, and LBCs of other assimilated groups.

Parallel ministry is difficult to implement. Some may object that it is not possible to implement parallel ministry because of their church's stage of growth or other practical problems. For example, the LBCs may all be children or there may not be enough working LBCs for them to be financially interdependent with the OBC congregation. In response, the issue then becomes making parallel ministry the goal and

---

[22] See chapter 2 for a discussion of the term "illusion of success."

[23] For a similar objection see: Richard B. Harms, *Paradigms from Luke–Acts for Multicultural Communities*, American University Studies. Series VII, Theology and Religion, vol. 216 (New York: Peter Lang, 2001), 87.

taking steps toward parallel ministry in part by educating the leaders and congregation about the biblical responsibility and necessity of working toward an Acts 6 parallel ministry. Ongoing education is important as immigration continues and people come and go from the congregation and the board/church leadership. Many LBC pastors have faced frustration because when they have finally convinced the OBC leadership of the necessity of parallel ministry, the board membership changes due to the natural end of leadership terms or a new wave of immigration brings new unassimilated OBCs into the church, and the education process needs to begin all over again. Similarly, OBC pastors and leaders often face frustration because they try to implement all or some aspects of parallel ministry and the LBC leaders make mistakes that compromise trust and hurt OBC feelings, thus making forgiveness and renewed education and commitment to parallel ministry necessary.

If all of the LBCs are children, then the church will not have an LBC pastor, but the church may make plans for parallel ministry by securing a worship service location that the children may use when they become youth and making sure the OBC congregation's expectation is for their youth to worship separately when they are older. The church may start looking for an LBC youth pastor when their children are getting ready to graduate into junior high. One possibility is recruiting a seminary student who will graduate about the same time the church's children are ready to enter the youth ministry. Many churches are unaware of the different types of resources and opportunities that seminaries provide to enable churches to make contact with students before they graduate.

If the LBC congregation has too few working people or all youth so that they cannot be financially interdependent, then the OBCs may take any number of steps to allow for the existing LBCs to have some measure of financial and decision-making authority. For example, the OBCs may create and deposit money in a separate bank account for the LBC congregation (the LBC staff, some LBC leader, or another appropriate person) to manage until the LBC congregation grows to the point that it can contribute to or meet its own financial obligations and/or contribute toward helping the OBC congregation.

Any practical problem may be overcome somehow; the issue is whether or not the goal is working toward the example of parallel ministry in Acts 6. For example, a rite of passage in American society is the handing over of the car keys by the parent to the child when they are old enough to drive, which brings with it significant freedom and responsibility. Parents may often tell their children they will give them the car keys when they are old enough to drive, while constantly reminding them that they are not old enough yet. However, if parents do not find out about the process of getting a driver's license ahead of time, do not let their children obtain a driver's permit, do not let them attend driver's education classes, and do not put in the time and energy to teach their children to drive, then their promise to hand over the keys at the appropriate time is, as it often is in reality in immigrant churches, an excuse not to hand over the financial and decision-making responsibility.

On the other hand, like driving for the first time, financial interdependence and even decision-making responsibility may be frightening as well as exciting for LBCs. LBCs must strive to step up to the challenges of Acts 6 when OBCs graciously offer them the opportunity. Historically, it has been easy for LBCs to blame their failures on OBC restrictions, while at the same time enjoying the security of OBC financial support. In Acts 6:7-13:3, after the Hebraists transferred the financial and decision-making authority, the Hellenists responsibly used them to grow the church despite difficult obstacles, and no doubt, any LBC ministry will face many intimidating obstacles even with the best OBC support. When the car keys are offered, gracious acceptance, responsible driving, and courage to face the new task are necessary.

Additional Reflections

Although the parallel ministry model is drawn from an explicit example in Scripture (Acts 6:1-7), not all readers may feel that their concerns regarding the model have been adequately assuaged. If this is the case, then readers may reflect on the following questions:

1. Do I find a specific error in the exegesis of Acts 6:1-7 given in chapter 2 or the in interpretation of the eleven points of parallel ministry from the passage?
2. Can I think of another biblical passage that more directly relates to the crisis of the immigrant church than Acts 6:1-7?
3. Even if my objection to parallel ministry has not been addressed or received an adequate response, does my objection undermine the biblical basis of parallel ministry?
4. Do I find parallel ministry to be biblical, yet I am still reluctant to implement it, and if so, then why?

5. Is my objection to parallel ministry based on biblical or cultural grounds?
6. Are there consequences or costs of parallel ministry of which I am afraid?
7. When I have found certain biblical commands or examples to be practically hard to obey or imitate in the past, how have I dealt with the discrepancy between my theology and practice?

The Acts 6:1-7 parallel ministry ecclesiastical structure is not a magic, instant solution to all of the problems of the immigrant church. However, it is a far more biblical solution that more adequately meets the concerns and needs raised in chapter 1 than any of the other past proposals to the specific crisis of the immigrant church. Consequently, parallel ministry gives your church the best chance at successfully meeting the needs of your congregation and reaching the lost. Implementing it will require sacrifice, hard work, changes in long held attitudes and dispositions (Acts 6:2, 5; Rom. 8:29; 2 Cor. 3:18), vision (Prov. 29:18, see KJV), and in many cases, forgiveness (Acts 6:1; Matt. 6:14-15) and reconciliation (Matt. 5:23-24; Acts 6:1) in addition to faith, prayer, and the work of the Triune God in all cases (Ps. 127:1).

Never forget that without the spiritual-relational dimension (Acts 6:2, 5) of parallel ministry, the ecclesiastical structure cannot stand (Acts 6:1-7). Conversely, as is the case in most immigrant churches, the best spiritual-relational intentions on the part of OBCs will not effectively meet the needs of LBCs and prevent them from being alienated from the church and their personal faith without the parallel ministry ecclesiastical structure. Many factors such as personality conflicts (Phil. 4:2-3), changing local economic conditions (Acts 16:16-19; 19:23-31), immigration rates, changes in the host culture, doctrinal divisions (Titus 3:9-10), poor leadership (1 Tim. 3:10), and all other forms of spiritual warfare that normally impact ministry (Luke 22:31; 2 Cor. 2:10-11; 1 Pet. 5:8), as well as God's plan for your church, may impact the successful implementation of the parallel ministry structure.

If parallel ministry is implemented, but does not seem to be resolving the crisis in your immigrant church, then either the spiritual-relational aspect has not been successfully implemented or some of these other factors may need to be addressed. When other underlying problems have been resolved, if the parallel ministry model of Acts 6:1-7 is faithfully imitated, then this ecclesiastical structure will provide an atmosphere that God may use (1 Cor. 3:6) for successfully meeting the needs of both your churched and unbelieving OBCs and LBCs (Acts 6:7; on this point see: "Table 2: An Unscientific LBC Congregational Survey" on the next page.).

Table 2: An Unscientific LBC Congregational Survey

The following table consists of questions taken from an annual congregational survey given to an LBC congregation after the board implemented the partial parallel ministry model in Table 2. The survey was completed and collected during the service. The approximate breakdown of those responding was comprised of: working adults (75 %), college and High School students (20%), and Junior High (5%). Although this survey is not scientific (it was not conducted using current sociological sampling criteria) and the demographic composition of the congregation is probably not typical of most LBC congregations in immigrant churches (most have mainly youth), nevertheless it seems likely that the results and the attitudes they suggest are representative of the LBCs of many immigrant churches. This table is offered as an illustration to aid in understanding and not as scientific sociological evidence to support any claim of this book.

Issue	Question	%Yes	%No	%N/A
Joint Services	Now that we no longer have joint services, will you be more inclined to bring unbelieving guests on major holidays such as Easter and Christmas?	85	7.5	7.5
Offering	Now that our English Speaking Group has "control" over our own finances (collecting our own offering and setting our own budget), do you expect it to positively affect your giving?	67	26	7
Leadership Participation	Now that we have a separate board meeting from the Taiwanese, would you be more inclined to serve on the leadership team as an Elder or a Deacon?	48	48	4

For Discussion

If 85% of the congregation is more likely to bring visitors if there are *no* joint services on the "most evangelistic" days of the year when people who only come to church once a year come, then what does this mean "joint" services are generally doing to church growth and congregational spiritual health?

If 67% of the congregation is willing to give more if they know that leaders from their own congregation are going to manage the money they give, then how is the physical unity of having one bank account impacting church growth and health?

Given that only a small percentage of the entire congregation will ever actually serve on the board, but 48% of the whole congregation would be more willing to serve if meetings were run in English and apart from immigrant congregation culture and issues, then what does that tell you about the impact of the physical unity of one board on the church's leadership and service potential and by implication church growth?

CHAPTER 4: Past Proposed Solutions

Ron Howard's 1995 film, "Apollo 13," popularized the ill-fated U.S. moon mission of that name for millions of Americans. As seen in the movie and as on all of the Apollo missions, a Saturn V rocket launched into space the "Apollo stack," composed of the command and service module or CSM and the lunar excursion module or LEM. For the Apollo 13 mission, the CSM was nicknamed Odyssey and the LEM was dubbed Aquarius. Unfortunately, due to a faulty installation, an oxygen tank exploded on the Odyssey and the crew of three astronauts (Jim Lovell, Fred Haise, and Jack Swigert) had to evacuate to the Aquarius. However, the Aquarius only had two carbon dioxide scrubbers (filters), which were only designed to handle two men for the time it took to make the trip to the moon and back in the Odyssey. The Aquarius' filters would not last long enough to get three astronauts all the way back to the earth. The Odyssey had extra filters, but they were square and the Aquarius' filters were round. The NASA scientists were stuck trying to figure out how to get a square peg to stick into a round hole using only the materials aboard Apollo 13, which consisted of plastic moon rock sample bags, spacesuit hoses, cardboard checklist covers, and duct tape.[1] The NASA scientists worked for two days straight trying all of the possible combinations of the materials to get the Odyssey's square filters to work with the Aquarius'

---

[1] *Encyclopedia Americana* Deluxe Library ed. (Danbury, CT: Grolier, 1997), s.v. "Apollo 13;" *The New Encyclopaedia Britannica* 15th ed. (Chicago: Encyclopaedia Britannica, 1993), s.v. "Apollo Program;" Jeffrey Kluger and James Lovell, *Apollo 13*, Reprint ed. (New York: Mariner Books, 2006), 87, 167, 188, 250, 255–58.

round filter slots. Fortunately for the Apollo 13 crew, NASA finally found the correct combination to insert a square peg into a round hole.

Less fortunately, pastors are still struggling with the logical combinations to get the differently shaped pieces of the immigrant church to work together to fit LBCs into the OBCs' slot and vice versa. This chapter introduces and describes the plastic, cardboard, and duct tape that pastors have been manipulating in a vain attempt to find a solution that will fit OBCs and LBCs together, much like the Odyssey's square peg into the Aquarius' round hole.

There are three main categories of solutions or ecclesiastical structures/models that have historically been proposed and implemented to resolve the crisis of the immigrant church: (1) bilingual worship, (2) separate worship services, and (3) church planting.[2] The names of these models may be different in various sources and some, such as Ortiz, may offer variations on the structures, but these three models are the main basic categories.[3] It is commonly recognized that these three models represent the typical stages of growth of immigrant churches.[4] However, not all

---

[2] William L. Eng, "Having an Effective Model for ABC Ministry within the Chinese Church," in *FACE* (Oakland, CA: Fellowship of American Chinese Evangelicals (FACE), 2009), 102;" Eddie Lo, "Body Life and Its Alternatives," in *ECCWE*, ed. Sharon Wai–Man Chan (Tsim Sha Tsui, Hong Kong: Chinese Coordination Centre of World Evangelism, 1986), 180–81; Mark Mullins, "The Life Cycle of Ethnic Churches in Sociological Perspective," *JJRS* 14, no. 4 (1987): 324; John L. Ng, "Church Models for Chinese Ministry," in *A Winning Combination: ABC/OBC: Understanding the Cultural Tensions in Chinese Churches*, ed. Cecilia Yau (Petaluma, CA: Chinese Christian Mission, 1986), 146–49; Peter Tow, "How to Solve the Linguistic Problem in the North American Chinese Church," in *ECCWE*, ed. Sharon Wai–Man Chan (Tsim Sha Tsui, Hong Kong: Chinese Coordination Centre of World Evangelism, 1986), 116–17.

[3] Manuel Ortiz, *The Hispanic Challenge: Opportunities Confronting the Church* (Downers Grove: InterVarsity, 1993), 117–22; Manuel Ortiz, *One New People: Models for Developing a Multiethnic Church*, Kindle ed. (Downers Grove: InterVarsity, 1996), K.l. 492–915.

[4] Kenneth P. Carlson, "Patterns in Development of the English Ministry in a Chinese Church," in *The 2008 Report: The Bay Area Chinese Churches Research Project Phase II*, ed. James Chuck and Timothy Tseng (Castro Valley, CA: The Institute for the Study of Asian American Christianity, 2009), 207–10; William L. Eng, "An Overview of Christian Work among ABCs," in *FACE* (Oakland, CA: FACE, 2009), 58–61; Ken Uyeda Fong, *Pursuing the Pearl: A Comprehensive Resource for Multi–Asian Ministry*, Updated ed. (Valley Forge, PA: Judson Press, 1999), 24; Mullins, "Ethnic Churches," 323–24. See also: Daniel A. Rodriguez, *A Future for the Latino Church: Models for Multilingual, Multigenerational Hispanic Congregations*, Kindle ed. (IVP Academic, 2011), K.l. 657–72. Significantly, Carlson lists the "Parallel

churches progress through each stage as some churches may skip steps, revert to previous steps, and/or never progress past a certain stage.[5]

This chapter introduces and describes these three models and the next chapter evaluates them. The general description of each model is followed by an explanation of several specific elements that help to define the models in more detail and characterize the church's stage of growth, including staffing structure, ruling board, demographics, relationship of OBCs and LBCs, OBC view of LBCs, form of unity, needs met, target group/vision of church, ownership, state of the cycle of tension. Table 3 at the end of this chapter contains a summary of all three models/stages of growth compared side by side and contrasted with the parallel ministry model.

Bilingual Worship

Most immigrant churches begin with a single monolingual worship service in the OBC language and move to some sort of bilingual format using both the OBC and LBC languages.[6] The service is bilingual in that some form of translation occurs, usually from the OBC to the LBC language. This may include (1) parallel translation from the pulpit, either through an interpreter with simultaneous translation in which the pastor speaks and then the translator immediately interprets each sentence or with a bilingual pastor translating for himself, (2) a translator whispering to a small group of LBCs in a section of the congregation, (3) translation over a speaker in a separate room, or (4) translation over headphones, usually with a reserved headphone section in the sanctuary.[7] At later stages of church growth, there may be an alternation of languages, such as using

---

Model," which is very similar to parallel minsitry, as the final stage of his sociological analysis. Carlson, "Patterns in Development," 209–10.

5 Eng, "Effective Model," 114.

6 Hyo Shick Pai, "Korean Congregational Church of Los Angeles: The Bilingual Ministry and Its Impact on Church Growth" (D.Ed.Min. diss., Fuller Theological Seminary, Pasadena, CA, 1987), 3, 10, 135. Some churches may even be trilingual or multilingual and may have multiple services with translation or merely with services in different languages. For example, it is not uncommon for some Chinese immigrant churches to use Mandarin, Cantonese, and English.

7 Tow, "Linguistic Problem," 116.

different languages for different parts of the service or using a different language on certain Sundays during the month or year.[8] It is likely that many churches have a bilingual worship service only, but some may attempt to run other ministries in a bilingual format.[9]

At this stage of the church's growth, the OBC pastor is the senior pastor and possibly the sole staff, although there may be a youth pastor and typically the church hires a secretary for the OBC pastor before even considering LBC staff. The church has a single ruling board with meetings held in the OBC language. The LBCs are dependent upon the OBCs. The OBCs are young parents and the LBCs are usually children. The OBCs view the LBCs as children. The church maintains a physical unity by having both OBCs and LBCs in the same service.[10] This model usually meets more of the needs of OBCs than LBCs. The church is typically focused on reaching OBCs and providing children's and/or youth ministries. The OBCs have a full sense of church ownership, and the LBCs are either unaware of ownership or are starting to become conscious of the concept. As the LBCs become older youth, the cycle of tension may start to build as they ask for a youth pastor and/or an LBC language service and the OBCs begin to fear the materializing assimilation process and perceived threat to family unity. The bilingual model is usually employed early in the lifecycle of an immigrant church, and the cycle of tension normally moves the church toward the separate service model.

Separate Worship Services

As the LBCs enter junior high, senior high, and college, many immigrant churches will hold separate worship services and Sunday school meetings in the OBC and LBC languages.[11] Depending on the number of people and the size of the facility, the two services may meet at

---

[8] Pai, "Bilingual Ministry," 142.

[9] David K. Chan, "Practical Ways of Increasing Understanding between Overseas–Born Chinese and Local–Born Chinese," in *ECCWE*, ed. Sharon Wai–Man Chan (Tsim Sha Tsui, Hong Kong: Chinese Coordination Centre of World Evangelism, 1986), 144; Pai, "Bilingual Ministry," 142, 200–01, 217.

[10] William L. Eng, "Church Programs That Minister Effectively to ABCs," in *FACE* (Oakland, CA: FACE, 2009), 144; Pai, "Bilingual Ministry," 142.

[11] Rodriguez calls these types of churches "multilingual, multigenerational" or "multiethnic, multigenerational" and he finds many of them to be positive examples. However, these types of churches are under the "illusion of success." Rodriguez, *Latino Church*, K.l. 139–41, 161–62, 543–44.

the same time or be staggered. If there is a youth or LBC associate pastor, the OBC senior pastor will frequently exert authority in the LBC service by preaching there periodically with or without translation, depending on his language ability.[12] Typically, there are "joint services" held on the major holidays in which the two services combine and so revert back to the bilingual model on these occasions.[13] Additionally, the church usually holds some "joint activities" that are commonly planned by the OBCs and may include an annual picnic, holiday meals, holiday performances by the LBCs, and outreach activities.[14] Some LBCs attempt to avoid attending the joint services and activities, and most think they are culturally irrelevant.[15]

At this stage of the church's growth, the OBC pastor is usually the senior pastor and frequently there is a youth pastor and/or an LBC associate pastor. In some rare instances, if the church retains this model for an extended period of time, the LBC may become the senior pastor.[16] The church has a single ruling board with meetings usually held in the

---

12 Fred Cheung, "Bridging Racial and Linguistic Gaps," in *ECCWE*, ed. Sharon Wai–Man Chan (Tsim Sha Tsui, Hong Kong: Chinese Coordination Centre of World Evangelism, 1986), 68; Steven J. Chin, "Reaching and Discipling Local–Born Chinese," in *ECCWE*, ed. Sharon Wai–Man Chan (Tsim Sha Tsui, Hong Kong: Chinese Coordination Centre of World Evangelism, 1986), 162.

13 Chin, "Local–Born Chinese," 162; Pyong Gap Min, *Preserving Ethnicity through Religion in America: Korean Protestants and Indian Hindus across Generations*, Kindle ed. (New York: New York University Press, 2010), K.l. 1799–1804.

14 Ernest Chan, "Appreciating Cultural Distinctives of the Local–Born Chinese," in *ECCWE*, ed. Sharon Wai–Man Chan (Tsim Sha Tsui, Hong Kong: Chinese Coordination Centre of World Evangelism, 1986), 107–08; Min, *Korean Protestants*, K.l. 3224–28; Kathleen Sullivan, "Catherine's Catholic Church: One Church, Parallel Congregations," in *Religion and the New Immigrants: Continuities and Adaptations*, Kindle ed., Helen Rose Ebaugh and Janet Saltzman Chafetz, eds. (Walnut Creek, CA: Altamira Press, 2000), p. 275.

15 Mercidieu Phillips, "Resolving the Causes of Second Generation Exodus from the Haitian Church in South Florida" (D.Ed.Min. diss., Bethel Seminary, Saint Paul, MN, 2011), 90; Rodriguez, *Latino Church*, K.l. 728–32.

16 William L. Eng and others, *FACE* (Oakland, CA: Fellowship of American Chinese Evangelicals (FACE), 2009), 57, 110–14; Phillips, "Haitian Church," 119; Rodriguez, *Latino Church*, K.l. 587–91.

OBC language and may have some LBC board members who are a numerical minority. The LBCs are dependent upon the OBCs. The OBCs are middle aged or mature adults and the LBCs are commonly youth, young adults, and/or young married couples. The OBCs view the LBCs as children and/or as rebellious teens. The church maintains a physical unity through the joint services and activities. In this model, more LBC needs are met than in the bilingual model, but the needs of OBCs tend to be primary. The church is typically focused on reaching OBCs and their children. The OBCs have a full sense of church ownership and the LBCs feel disenfranchised. At this stage, the cycle of tension is building to a climax as the church typically has lost many of its LBC young adults and may have few, if any, young LBC married couples. Commonly, conflict occurs and tension builds as the LBCs wish to change the church's name to reach other groups besides OBCs, have more representation on the board in order to get approval for and fund their ministry projects, and to have more control over human resource issues regarding their pastoral staff. This tension typically pushes the church toward the silent exodus or a church split or plant.

The main difference between the separate service and parallel ministry models is that the former has not transferred financial and decision making authority from the OBCs to the LBCs so that they may create a culturally relevant ministry. Many immigrant churches falsely think that they are running a parallel ministry when they have an LBC pastor, LBCs on their church board, and a sizeable LBC congregation. However, they are under the illusion of success and only have a separate service because they have not transferred financial and decision-making authority as evidenced in part through their emphasis on being "one church" in the unbiblical manner of stressing physical over spiritual unity (Eph. 4:2-6). This may be exasperated by highlighting the necessity of one vision, one mission, one message, one board, one ethnic name, and one (bilingual) website. Even if all of the structural elements of parallel ministry described in chapters 2 and 3 are implemented, but in the spiritual-relational aspect, the OBCs have not truly transferred decision-making authority to the LBCs, then regardless of the ecclesiastical structure, that church merely has a separate service (partial parallel ministry) rather than a full biblical parallel ministry. In such a case, the cycle of tension will inevitably, as it historically has done for over two hundred years of immigrant church history in the United States, lead to eventual church death, a church split, or a church plant.

Church Planting

When the cycle of tension reaches its peak, there is usually one of three outcomes: a mass second generation exodus, a church split, or a church plant. The hostile church split and the amicable church plant both generally result in the same type of model, which is a separate independent LBC church. The degree of separation and continued communication between the new LBC church and the originating OBC church is not necessarily dependent upon whether the new church is a split or plant. Frequently, the new LBC church will physically relocate to a new facility. In both cases, the originating OBC church often must rebuild its separate LBC worship service. Although some LBC church plants may occur as independent startups that do not originate from an OBC church as a split or plant, the founding pastor in these cases is typically an LBC who left a position in an OBC church because the OBC leaders did not transfer financial and decision-making power.[17]

As a separate independent church, the LBC church has its own staff and board. The LBCs are completely independent from the OBCs, except in the case of a church plant in which case some financial dependence and accountability may exist for the first few years. At this stage, typically the OBCs are mature adults and the LBCs are commonly youth, young adults, and/or young married couples. The OBCs view the LBCs as ungrateful children.[18] The churches have little or no unity and are possibly hostile toward each other. In this model, the needs of LBCs are primarily met and the needs of OBCs are secondary or unmet. The OBC church is typically focused on reaching OBCs and their children and the new LBC church commonly focuses on reaching LBCs and/or being multi-ethnic. The OBCs and LBCs feel a sense of ownership over their respective ministries. At this stage, the cycle of tension has been broken

---

[17] Russell Jeung, *Faithful Generations: Race and New Asian American Churches*, Kindle ed. (New Brunswick, NJ: Rutgers University Press, 2005), K.l. 897–98, 1005–07, 1010–11, 2232–33; Eng, "Overview," 70. See also: Fong, *Multi–Asian Ministry*, 197; Samuel Ling and Clarence Cheuk, *The "Chinese" Way of Doing Things: Perspectives on American–Born Chinese and the Chinese Church in North America* (Phillipsburg, NJ: P & R Publishing, 1999), 61, 109, 135–36; Phillips, "Haitian Church," 12–13, 170–72.

[18] Phillips, "Haitian Church," 173.

for the LBCs, but the tension often remains and is heightened in the OBC church. Table 3 on the next page contains a summary of all three models/stages of growth compared side by side and contrasted with the parallel ministry model.

Now that the three basic ecclesiastical structures that have been historically proposed and practiced have been described, the next section will evaluate both the models themselves and the proposals made in their favor.

Table 3: Comparison of Models of Ministry/Stages of Church Growth

	Bi-lingual Worship	Separate Services	Church Planting	Parallel Ministry
Staffing Structure	OBC Sr. Pastor	OBC Sr. Pastor LBC Youth and/or Associate Pastor	OBC Sr. Pastor LBC Sr. Pastor	OBC and LBC co-pastors
Ruling Board	OBC board, OBC language used	OBC majority board, possibly translation	Separate boards	OBC and LBC boards are interdependent
Demographics	OBCs are young parents LBCs are young children	OBCs are middle aged and mature adults LBC are mostly youth	OBCs are mature adults LBCs are young adults and young couples	OBCs are mature adults LBCs are young adults and young couples
Relationship of OBCs and LBCs	LBCs dependent on OBCs	LBCs dependent on OBCs	OBCs and LBCs are both independent	OBCs and LBCs are interdependent
OBC view of LBCs	OBCs view the LBCs as children	OBCs view the LBCs as children and/or as rebellious teens	OBCs view the LBCs as ungrateful children	Mutual respect
Form of Unity	Physical unity, all in same service	Physical unity, joint services and activities	No unity and possibly hostility	Spiritual unity
Needs Met	More OBC needs met	OBCs needs primary LBCs needs secondary	OBCs needs are unmet Some LBCs needs met	OBCs and LBCs meet each others needs
Vision	Reaching OBCs and their LBC children	OBCs focus on OBCs and their LBC children LBCs focus on LBCs and maybe multiethnic	OBCs focus on OBCs and their LBC children LBCs focus on LBCs and maybe multiethnic	OBCs focus on OBCs and their LBC children LBCs focus on LBCs and maybe multiethnic
Ownership	OBCs have ownership LBCs unaware or developing the concept	OBCs have ownership LBCs feel disenfranchised	OBCs and LBCs have full ownership over their respective churches	OBCs and LBCs have full ownership over their respective congregations

CHAPTER 5: Deficiencies of Past Proposals

In today's electronics-based world, it is possible that at least some younger readers are unfamiliar with the cardboard and plastic board games of the past generations—except as they have been reimagined into their software-based counterparts. One such game that has made its way into adventure, action-adventure, and puzzle computer games is the jigsaw puzzle.[1] A jigsaw puzzle might be recognized either from its board or electronic version as being a puzzle consisting of "irregularly cut pieces that are to be fitted together to form a picture."[2] In the old cardboard versions, as one shuffled the physical pieces around on a table to try to form the picture, the situation might be complicated by human error. For instance, if two puzzles were being played by someone else beforehand, that person may have mixed some of the pieces together when placing them back into the boxes. Other times, one of the pieces may have fallen on the floor under the table when the puzzle was poured out of the box. In either of these cases, finishing the puzzle was far more complicated and sometimes even impossible to accomplish—the picture just could not be correctly formed.

---

[1] J. P. Wolf, "Genre and the Video Game,' in *The Medium of the Video Game*, ed. J. P. Wolf (Austin, TX: University of Texas, 2001), 113–34.

[2] Merriam–Webster's Collegiate Dictionary, 11th ed., s.v. "jigsaw puzzle."

The three disparate church models presented in the last chapter (bilingual, separate service, and church planting) are like three different attempts to shuffle the pieces around to solve the crisis and form a working picture of the immigrant church. However, in some cases, the various models are using pieces from two different puzzles, sociology and theology, to solve the puzzle. In other cases, some of the models have dropped a piece on the floor or at least put it in the wrong place and have left out the Bible or failed to give the Scriptures their due place as the final authority in solving the puzzle. This chapter will explain how the past proposals of these three different models provide deficient solutions to the jigsaw puzzle that is the crisis of the immigrant church.

Each of the three disparate models presented has historical proponents and practitioners, but all three are deficient solutions to the crisis of the immigrant church both in theoretical proposal and actual practice. While all of the proposals have a deficient biblical basis, some of the proposals are deficient because they merely describe, rather than solve, the problem (Ling, Zaki), compromise their biblical basis with sociological-cultural qualifications (ECCWE, FACE, Ortiz, Phillips, Rodriguez), and/or combine a sociological-cultural basis with a counterproductive solution (Fong, Jeung, Pai).

The biblical basis of the arguments made by the majority of the past proposals are deficient because they involve invalid analogies. An analogy is a "comparison made between one thing and another for the purpose of explanation or clarification.... The process of arguing from similarity in known respect to similarity in other respects; the use of parallel cases as a basis for reasoning."[3] "Analogies rely on the fact that there is some point of comparison which links the two or more things in the analogy" or comparison.[4] The analogies used by the various proponents of the past proposals are invalid because they use biblical passages that involve issues other than ecclesiology (church structure) and

---

[3] Michael Proffitt, ed. *The Oxford English Dictionary Online* (Oxford: Oxford University, June 2016 [on–line]. Accessed 19 August 2016. Available from http://www.oed.com/view/Entry/7030?redirectedFrom=analogy&; Internet), s.v. "analogy, n."

[4] Matthew Taylor and Jill Oliphant, *OCR Philosophy of Religion for AS and A2*, ed. Jon Mayled, 3rd ed. (New York: Routledge, 2015), 396.

its relation to resolving the crisis of the immigrant church. Their analogies fail because the "point of comparison" between the biblical texts they select and the contemporary situation they are trying to solve is not sufficiently similar. In terms of a common American colloquialism, they are comparing apples to oranges rather than apples to apples.

Not only do the past proposals have deficient biblical bases, but they also have bases in sociology that either undermine or overshadow the biblical rationales offered. In various ways and to different degrees, all of the past proposals, not only use sociology to define the problem, but also to provide the solution to the crisis for the immigrant church and so compromise the authority and sufficiency of Scripture. Although in sociology, as Meeker claims, "there is no generally accepted definition," the *Oxford English Dictionary* offers a comprehensive definition of sociology that encompasses many of the different aspects of the broad field: "The study of the development, structure, and functioning of human society."[5]

The sociological elements involved in the arguments surrounding the crisis of the immigrant church may include, but are not limited to, culture, case study approaches, demographic studies, contemporary missiology, or church growth principles. While some of the sociological elements used for support in the past proposals for the various ministry models may not be necessarily biblically inconsistent (however some are), the Bible, rather than sociology, is the ultimate authority for the church (2 Tim. 3:16-17). Sociology may be useful in examining the contemporary situation in order to define the problems the church is facing, but the Bible must provide the solutions for the church as its authoritative guide for faith and life.

The following sub-sections focus primarily on the proposals by the most prominent proponents of each of the three ecclesiastical models: bilingual service (Pai), separate service (FACE), and church planting

---

[5] Barbara F. Meeker, "Sociology," in *The Concise Encyclopedia of Sociology*, ed. George Ritzer and J. Michael Ryan (Malden, MA: Wiley–Blackwell, 2011), 599; Michael Proffitt, ed. *The Oxford English Dictionary Online* (Oxford: Oxford University, June 2016 [on–line]. Accessed 19 August 2016. Available from http://www.oed.com/view/Entry/7030?redirectedFrom= analogy &; Internet), s.v. "sociology, n." On the lack of an accepted definition for sociology and an attempt to unify the disparate meanings see: Vidya Bhushan and D. R. Sachdeva, *Fundamentals of Sociology* (Delhi, India: Pearson, 2012), 4–5.

(Fong).[6] Although an unpublished doctor of ministry dissertation, Pai's formal proposal for bilingual ministry seems to be one of the longest of such defenses in print, the only one to provide biblical support for the view, and is far more comprehensive than those in the ECCWE material. The *FACE Handbook* has the most comprehensive and cogent argument in print for what they believe is parallel ministry, but what is in reality a separate worship service or a partial parallel ministry. The *Handbook* is written by a panel of five distinguished veteran pastors with decades of ministry experience. Ken Fong's work is a revision of his doctor of ministry dissertation that argues for the church planting model. He is locally renowned in California as the pastor of the successful Evergreen Church in Los Angeles and is nationally recognized as being a prominent leader in the Asian American community. Each proposal is briefly described, analyzed for deficiencies, and finally the historical strengths and weakness of each model are evaluated.

Bilingual Worship

One of the seemingly few proponents of bilingual ministry in print is Pai with his doctor of ministry dissertation, "Korean Congregational Church of Los Angeles: The Bilingual Ministry and Its Impact on Church Growth." Pai's thesis is that "bilingual ministry is the most effective ministry," as opposed to monolingual ministry, for implementing the principles of the church growth movement in the immigrant church.[7] Pai argues that it is the nature of the church to grow

[6] Hyo Shick Pai, "Korean Congregational Church of Los Angeles: The Bilingual Ministry and Its Impact on Church Growth" (D.Ed.Min. diss., Fuller Theological Seminary, Pasadena, CA, 1987). Cp. David K. Chan, "Practical Ways of Increasing Understanding between Overseas–Born Chinese and Local–Born Chinese," in *ECCWE*, ed. Sharon Wai–Man Chan (Tsim Sha Tsui, Hong Kong: Chinese Coordination Centre of World Evangelism, 1986), 143–44; Moses Chow and David T. Chow, "Practical Cooperation Programs and Projects between Overseas–Born Chinese and Local–Born Chinese," in *ECCWE*, ed. Sharon Wai–Man Chan (Tsim Sha Tsui, Hong Kong: Chinese Coordination Centre of World Evangelism, 1986), 150–52. David K. Woo, "Introduction," in *FACE* (Oakland, CA: FACE, 2009), 9–10. Ken Uyeda Fong, *Pursuing the Pearl: A Comprehensive Resource for Multi–Asian Ministry*, Updated ed. (Valley Forge, PA: Judson Press, 1999), x, 1.

[7] Pai, "Bilingual Ministry," 33–34, 220.

(according to the church growth movement), but the cultural conflict in the immigrant church is hindering growth.[8] In order to overcome the hindrance of cultural conflicts and begin to grow numerically and spiritually, the church should imitate Jesus in becoming bilingual or multilingual by implementing bilingual worship services and other types of bilingual ministries.[9]

Pai's biblical support for bilingual ministry is deficient, because he uses an invalid analogy by making a descriptive and incidental textual detail normative for church practice by means of implication rather than recommending that the church follow an explicit principle or example in the Scripture that is central to the meaning of a particular passage and has to do with ecclesiology (the structure of church government in relation to cultural conflicts). According to Pai, Jesus was at least bilingual, speaking Hebrew (Luke 4:16-17; Rev. 9:11; 16:16) and Aramaic (Matt. 27:46; Mark 15:34; Luke 23:46), and may have been multilingual, also speaking Latin (Matt. 27:1-25) and Greek (John 19:19-21).[10] Pai implies that since Jesus was at least bilingual, then both OBCs and LBCs should imitate Him and become bilingual.[11] Pai's implication rests heavily on his argument that language is an unavoidable part of ministry as the means of communication of the Gospel and God's will.[12] The implied idea seems to be that since language is necessary for ministry and since Jesus was bilingual/multilingual, then the ministry of believers should be bilingual.

However, Pai's solution rests on an invalid analogy, because Jesus' bilingual ability is an incidental and descriptive detail in the biblical text for which there is no explicit command to imitate, particularly to imitate for the purpose of resolving cultural tensions in the church. Such imitation seems less comparable to obeying the explicit command of emulating Jesus' love (John 13:1, 15, 34-35) and more comparable to the optional or even trivial act of copying His trade as a carpenter (Matt. 13:55; Mark 6:3).

Furthermore, Pai's analogy is invalid because he mistakes a linguistic issue for an ecclesiological one. Even if one allows that contemporary believers should imitate Jesus in being bilingual, speaking

---

[8] Ibid., 33, 88–96.

[9] Ibid., 62, 72–73, 127–28, 142.

[10] Ibid., 62, 72–73, 127–28.

[11] Ibid., 127–28.

[12] Ibid., 69, 86.

more than one language does not necessitate a certain model of ministry or structure of church government. For example, the preceding proposal for parallel ministry demonstrated that the biblical evidence may even be against bilingual ministry as Acts 6:1 and 9 imply that Hebraic and Hellenistic Christian Jews were bilingual but met separately for worship.

Not only is Pai's biblical basis deficient because he uses an invalid biblical analogy, but his main rational for using a bilingual model is, in fact, not biblical, but rather sociological. In Pai's thesis section, he never mentions the idea of imitating a bilingual or multilingual Jesus, but rather stresses that bilingual ministry is important so that both OBCs and LBCs can assimilate each other's respective cultures.[13] In fact, in Pai's overall argument, the rationale of running a bilingual ministry as a form of imitating the multilingual Jesus, is eclipsed in terms of both space and importance by the sociological benefits of mutual assimilation by both OBCs and LBCs through becoming bilingual and running a bilingual ministry model.[14] Pai's argument has a primarily sociological basis and a deficient biblical basis resting on an invalid analogy.

Although there are some advantages to bilingual ministry, this model is actually a counterproductive and biblically inconsistent solution to the crisis of the immigrant church. Pai is correct that bilingual ministry may help OBCs assimilate into the host culture by helping them learn the native language.[15] It is also true that bilingual ministry is likely more effective for LBCs than monolingual ministry in the OBC language.[16] Perhaps the most important practical benefit of bilingual ministry is that it addresses the OBC concern of keeping the church together as a family by preserving physical unity through a worship service in which OBCs and LBCs are sitting in the same room.[17] However, there are many disadvantages of bilingual ministry:

---

[13] Ibid., 33–34.

[14] Ibid., 33–34, 131–39, 213.

[15] Ibid., 135.

[16] Ibid., 134.

[17] Chan, "Increasing Understanding," 144; Pai, "Bilingual Ministry," 142, 208.

1. Simultaneous translation is time consuming.
2. It is difficult to get bilingual leaders and/or translators.
3. It is expensive to hire bilingual leaders/translators, to buy equipment such as earphones, or to build a translation room in the church.
4. Whichever group is receiving translation feels like "second-class citizens."[18]

Bilingual ministry overcomes the language barrier, but fails to overcome the cultural barrier by presenting a worship service, sermon, and music, that are culturally irrelevant to the group receiving the translation. Moreover, bilingual ministry historically has failed not only to provide a culturally relevant ministry to LBCs, but even most OBCs find it ineffective to meet their needs other than that of physically keeping the family together (Acts 6:1).[19] Since bilingual ministry views the church as a hierarchy, then it only allows for a single patriarchal leader/senior pastor and board. Consequently, this model does not alleviate the fear of some OBCs that bilingual-bicultural LBCs leaders will replace them. It also does not alleviate the fear of some OBC lay leaders, who have replaced the lost professional and political prestige they held in their home country with their leadership position in the church, that they will not lose their newfound status to LBCs who join the church board. Only by having co-pastors (Acts 6:2-6; 20:28; 1 Pet. 5:2-4; Heb. 13:20) and separate boards with equal authority (Acts 6:2-4, 6) does the parallel ministry model alleviate the twin fears of replacement and loss of status. Decisively, not only have proponents of bilingual ministry failed to provide adequate biblical support for their model, but parallel ministry as pictured in Acts 6:1-7 contradicts the bilingual ministry model.

---

[18] Pai, "Bilingual Ministry," 218–19; Daniel A. Rodriguez, *A Future for the Latino Church: Models for Multilingual, Multigenerational Hispanic Congregations*, Kindle ed. (IVP Academic, 2011), K.l. 728–32.

[19] Steven J. Chin, "Reaching and Discipling Local–Born Chinese," in *ECCWE*, ed. Sharon Wai–Man Chan (Tsim Sha Tsui, Hong Kong: Chinese Coordination Centre of World Evangelism, 1986), 163; Rodriguez, *Latino Church*, K.l. 728–32; Peter Tow, "How to Solve the Linguistic Problem in the North American Chinese Church," in *ECCWE*, ed. Sharon Wai–Man Chan (Tsim Sha Tsui, Hong Kong: Chinese Coordination Centre of World Evangelism, 1986), 115–16.

Separate Worship Services

In *Completing the Face of the Chinese Church in America* [*FACE Handbook*], several of the directors of the Fellowship of American Chinese Evangelicals (FACE) created a handbook for LBC ministry with the expressed purpose "to assist Chinese churches and their leaders to increase the effectiveness of their ministries to ABCs" (American-Born Chinese).[20] Yuen adeptly summarizes the five main points of the book as requirements for an effective LBC ministry, and the second of these is that there must be an effective ministry model or ecclesiastical structure.[21]

While the FACE proposal is an excellent work that is the most comprehensive, cogent, and biblically based argument for an ecclesiastical model, it has several deficiencies:

1. Its analysis of Acts 6:1-7 misses some key components of parallel ministry.
2. It claims to be promoting parallel ministry, but it is only promoting a *partial* parallel ministry that really amounts to a separate service model.
3. It inconsistently defines parallel ministry.
4. It ultimately allows sociology rather than the Bible to be the final arbiter of normative church practice.

First, among other points, Wong astutely recognizes that the cultural conflict in Acts 6:1-7 serves as a valid analogy for resolving the crisis in the immigrant church and that the conflict was resolved through an ecclesiological solution by transferring decision-making authority.[22] However, as chapter 2 demonstrated, Wong overlooks several key points in the passage that are essential components of parallel ministry, such as

---

[20] Peter Yuen, "Effectively Promoting Missions among ABC Christians," in *FACE* (Oakland, CA: FACE, 2009), 151.

[21] Ibid., 151.

[22] Joseph C. Wong, "The Biblical Basis for Promoting Effective ABC Ministries," in *FACE* (Oakland, CA: FACE, 2009), 19–20. For similar analyses with the same deficiencies see: Mercidieu Phillips, "Resolving the Causes of Second Generation Exodus from the Haitian Church in South Florida" (D.Ed.Min. diss., Bethel Seminary, Saint Paul, MN, 2011), 31–32; Rodriguez, *Latino Church*, K.l. 97–136.

the observation that financial authority (Acts 6:2) was transferred as well as decision-making authority (Acts 6:3-6).

Second, since Wong does not identify all of the essential elements of parallel ministry from Acts 6:1-7, then the *FACE Handbook* really argues for a separate service or partial parallel ministry model.[23] In a separate service or partial parallel ministry model, among other things, financial and decision-making authority are not completely transferred so that the needs of both OBCs and LBCs are not adequately met (Acts 6:1) as they are when all of the elements of Acts 6:1-7 are considered and implemented in a full parallel ministry model.

Third, the *FACE Handbook* inconsistently defines parallel ministry. For example, Eng seems to allow that the various elements of Acts 6 are optional, depending on the circumstances, by claiming that in "parallel ministries….Each *may* have its own leadership and pastorate…*may* share…a common budget."[24] Wong, on the other hand, insists that for "a church to develop a parallel ministry, it *must* have equivalent…indigenous pastoral leaders and lay leaders."[25] Consequently, Eng seems to view co-pastors and separate budgets as optional, while Wong argues that they are necessary.

When one looks to proponents of parallel ministry outside of the *FACE Handbook*, the situation is no less confusing as parallel ministry is described as the separate service model. For example, Chin contradicts Eng and Wong by claiming that parallel ministry must be maintained by having "one senior pastor, one budget, and one board of deacons."[26] Furthermore, Wong and Eng seem to define parallel ministry in terms of a change in attitude and ecclesiastical structure, while Ling and Yuen depict parallel ministry as being more "comprehensive" in the sense of entailing all areas of ministry (not only a worship service, but also fellowship, discipleship, etc.) to "every age group in the church" (as opposed to LBC ministry focusing only on children and youth).[27] Ling also emphasizes

---

[23] William L. Eng, "Having an Effective Model for ABC Ministry within the Chinese Church," in *FACE* (Oakland, CA: Fellowship of American Chinese Evangelicals (FACE), 2009), 103–08.

[24] Emphasis added. Ibid., 107.

[25] Joseph C. Wong, "Culturally–Sensitive OBC Leadership," in *FACE* (Oakland, CA: Fellowship of American Chinese Evangelicals (FACE), 2009), 86.

[26] Chin, "Local–Born Chinese," 162.

[27] Eng, "Effective Model," 103–08; Samuel Ling and Clarence Cheuk, *The "Chinese" Way of Doing Things: Perspectives on American–Born Chinese and the Chinese*

individual spiritual-relational change and downplays corporate structural change.[28] While there are elements of truth in Eng, Wong, and Ling's definitions, chapters 2 and 3 argued that Acts 6:1-7 provides a normative definition of parallel ministry that eliminates such inconsistent definitions.

Finally, the FACE presentation ultimately undermines the biblical basis presented in Acts 6:1-7 in at least two ways. One way is that the later authors do not tie their points back to Wong's analysis of Acts 6 by parenthetical Scripture citation, and so at times, they stray from the points in Acts 6.

Another way Acts 6 loses its normative force in the *FACE Handbook* is that several of the authors argue the sociological spectrum of assimilation (the idea that people are at different levels of assimilation) requires various ecclesiastical models for groups with different levels of assimilation.[29] In addition to assimilation, at least part of the concern expressed by the FACE authors is trying to take into account practical factors that may impact the implementation of parallel ministry such as finances, staffing, and geography. But the handbook as a whole also provides solutions for these practical obstacles, such as volunteer staff to overcome financial limitations, staff from the host culture when LBC staff cannot be found, and planting LBC churches in communities that are too far from OBC churches and have no OBCs.[30] In this last geographic case, Acts 6 does not apply because there is no conflict between LBCs and OBCs.

Church in North America (Phillipsburg, NJ: P & R Publishing, 1999), xviii, 206–07; Joseph Wong, "Dealing with Tensions in a Bi–Cultural Church," in *ECCWE*, ed. Sharon Wai–Man Chan (Tsim Sha Tsui, Hong Kong: Chinese Coordination Centre of World Evangelism, 1986), 148; Peter Yuen, "Parallel Ministries," in *ECCWE*, ed. Sharon Wai–Man Chan (Tsim Sha Tsui, Hong Kong: Chinese Coordination Centre of World Evangelism, 1986), 145.

28 Ling and Cheuk, *The "Chinese" Way of Doing Things*, xviii, 206–07.

29 Eng, "Effective Model," 110, 119; Wayland Wong, "Who Are the American–Born Chinese?," in *FACE* (Oakland, CA: FACE, 2009), 28–31, 47; David K. Woo, "Planting ABC Churches," in *FACE* (Oakland, CA: FACE, 2009), 161–62.

30 Eng, "Effective Model," 109–110, 119; David K. Woo, "Planting ABC Churches," 161–63.

Outside the *FACE Handbook*, Ng similarly argues that different levels of assimilation or the cultural spectrum requires different models and adds that to ignore this sociological issue is "culturally naïve."[31] However, the cultural spectrum argument is both practically and theologically deficient. Practically, the argument ignores the fact that, historically, the various existing models, with the exception of parallel ministry, have failed to stop the second-generation exodus. Theologically, the argument that size, resources, or other practical factors change the goal of parallel ministry (Acts 6:1-7) not only makes sociology rather than the Bible (Acts 6) normative, but it is also akin to the argument that since people lack the resources to avoid lying, then truth telling should no longer be the goal (Col. 3:9). People may fail to live up to biblical standards due to a lack of knowledge (Lev. 4:27–28; Luke 12:48) or power (Rom. 5:6, 7:18-20, 8:3), but such failure does not change the moral standard. In a similar way, chapter 3 argued that since the moral standard in Acts 6:1-7 is parallel ministry, then size, resources, or other practical factors do not change that goal or standard.

There are three major historic objections to the separate service model and one biblical objection.[32] All of these objections apply to the parallel ministry model as well as the separate service model, because the separate service model is really a partial parallel ministry.

It breaks up families. The most common objection to parallel ministry, whether the partial separate service or the full version, is that it breaks up families by physically dividing them.[33] While there is some truth to this objection, it is historically and biblically incorrect. Historically, it is not parallel ministry that separates families, but rather the failure to implement parallel ministry that has separated families. This is because the church's use of deficient and biblically inconsistent ecclesiastical models has resulted in the silent exodus and caused LBCs to

---

[31] John L. Ng, "Church Models for Chinese Ministry," in *A Winning Combination: ABC/OBC: Understanding the Cultural Tensions in Chinese Churches*, ed. Cecilia Yau (Petaluma, CA: Chinese Christian Mission, 1986), 145.

[32] Among numerous and other less serious objections is that of logistics, such as space and timing. Most churches accommodate separate services by either staggering their service times, by rearranging their current facility space, or in extreme cases, moving to or building a new space. Pai, "Bilingual Ministry," 208; Yuen, "Parallel Ministries," 146.

[33] William L. Eng, "An Overview of Christian Work among ABCs," in *FACE* (Oakland, CA: FACE, 2009), 60; Pai, "Bilingual Ministry," 208; Rodriguez, *Latino Church*, K.l. 724–25; Tow, *Linguistic Problem*, 117; Yuen, "Parallel Ministries," 145.

fall away from the faith.[34] Biblically, the Bible does not commend physical unity as evidence of true worship (worshipping in the same physical location, John 4:19–24), but does command theological unity (belief in the same doctrine as described in Ephesians 4:4-6) and spiritual unity (forgiveness to maintain relationships as explained in Ephesians 4:2-3).[35] Parallel ministry sacrifices *some* physical unity to preserve the more important spiritual unity (Eph. 4:2-3).

It causes church splits. The second most common objection to separate services is that it will cause a church split.36 Typically, the thinking fears that LBCs will split the church by making a power grab.37 In truth, however, the separate service model merely delays this split while parallel ministries will actually prevent church splits by diffusing the cycle of tension and meeting the needs of LBCs.38 Yuen claims, "There have been no actual splits taking place in the churches in America caused by parallel services."39 In a sense, Yuen is incorrect because separate services or partial parallel ministries only prolong the outcome of church splits by meeting more LBC needs, but eventually, LBCs will leave if a full Acts 6 parallel ministry is not implemented that meets the needs of both LBCs and OBCs.

The separate service model does meet some LBC needs for a culturally relevant ministry (Acts 6:1) by transferring some decision-making authority (Acts 6:2-6), but a partial parallel ministry does not meet the needs of LBCs (Acts 6:1), because the model fails to transfer financial authority (Acts 6:2), allow for a culturally relevant ministry vision (Acts 6:1), and transfer staffing control (Acts 6:3, 5).[40] As a result, the separate

---

[34] For a similar judgment see: Tow, "Linguistic Problem," 117; Woo, "Introduction," 8; Yuen, "Parallel Ministries," 145.

[35] For a similar judgment see: Woo, "Introduction," 23; Yuen, "Parallel Ministries," 145–46.

[36] Eng, "Overview," 60–62; Yuen, "Parallel Ministries," 145–46.

[37] Wong, "American–Born Chinese," 47.

[38] Ibid., 48.

[39] Yuen, "Parallel Ministries," 145–46.

[40] For the idea that LBCs need a culturally relevant vision or mission see the interpretation of Acts 6:1 in chapters 2 and 3. For a similar judgment see: Mark

service model only delays the exodus and a church split/plant by temporarily easing, but not diffusing, the cycle of tension. Furthermore, this model historically has the danger that some OBCs may leave the church because they oppose the changes or because the changes are implemented poorly.[41]

LBC services are hard to staff. Another weakness of the separate service model is that LBC services are hard to staff due to a lack of LBC leaders and/or church finances.[42] Eng responds that the church can start with volunteers, such as seminary interns, to overcome lack of finances, and Yuen responds that staff from the host culture can help minister until the church can raise up LBC leaders.[43] While the number of available LBC leaders is likely higher for many post-1965 immigrant groups today in America than in the past, Wong notes that, for a number of reasons, LBCs would rather minister in LBC than OBC churches.[44] This lack of desire may be overcome by promoting a full parallel ministry model to potential LBC ministry candidates.

Acts 6 is not parallel, but rather multicultural. A final and biblical objection against separate services comes from Chan. He argues that the early church did not resolve the cultural conflict between Hebraic and Hellenistic Jews (OBCs and LBCs) in Acts 6:1-7 by setting up "two parallel congregations," but as in the Antioch church "they integrated these two cultural groups [Acts 11:19-20] and formed a team of multi-cultural leaders to work together [Acts 13:1]."45 However, Chan's

---

Mullins, "The Life Cycle of Ethnic Churches in Sociological Perspective," *JJRS* 14, no. 4 (1987): 325, 327; Manuel Ortiz, *The Hispanic Challenge: Opportunities Confronting the Church* (Downers Grove: InterVarsity, 1993), 123–24; Phillips, "Haitian Church," 125, 152–53; Rodriguez, *Latino Church*, K.l. 568–72.

[41] Phillips, "Haitian Church," 141; Rodriguez, *Latino Church*, K.l. 614–16, 739–42.

[42] Ling and Cheuk, *Chinese Way*, xviii–xix, 102–04; Wong, "Culturally–Sensitive," 71; Yuen, "Parallel Ministries," 146.

[43] Eng, "Effective Model," 109–10; William L. Eng, "Church Programs That Minister Effectively to ABCs," in *FACE* (Oakland, CA: FACE, 2009), 129; Yuen, "Parallel Ministries," 146.

[44] Franklin Lee, "How to Encourage and Train More Local–Born Chinese Ministers," in *ECCWE*, ed. Sharon Wai–Man Chan (Tsim Sha Tsui, Hong Kong: Chinese Coordination Centre of World Evangelism, 1986), 158; Wong, "Future Need," 172–73.

[45] David K. Chan, "Church Planting in Multi–Cultural Situation," in *ECCWE*, ed. Sharon Wai–Man Chan (Tsim Sha Tsui, Hong Kong: Chinese Coordination Centre of World Evangelism, 1986), 173–74.

objection is mistaken, because he overlooks at least two crucial textual features.First, Chan conflates the Jerusalem church in Acts 6:7 with the Antiochene church in Acts 13:1, apparently because Stephen is mentioned in both places (Acts 6:5; Acts 13:1). Consequently, Chan overlooks the parallel ministry solution to the cultural conflict in Acts 6:2-6 and replaces it with the multicultural leadership situation in Acts 13:1. Chan may be thinking that the list of the seven leaders in Acts 6:5 in itself or the seven leaders combined with the apostles represents a multiethnic or multicultural leadership team/church, but with the exception of Nicolas, the seven are probably all Hellenistic Jews (Acts 6:5). Furthermore, while the seven leaders (Acts 6:5) and the apostles differed culturally in being Hellenists and Hebraists (Acts 6:1), they were both ethnically Jews and were on separate leadership teams overseeing different ministry areas, specifically the widows' distribution (Acts 6:2–3) and prayer and the Word (Acts 6:4). Therefore, a single multicultural board, as exists in some contemporary churches with a bilingual or separate service model, did not exist in the Jerusalem church as Chan implies.

Second, Chan overlooks the fact that the two passages not only represent different narrative and geographic circumstances, but that they also represent two different demographic situations. In Acts 6, the Jerusalem church consisted of Hebraic Jews and Hellenistic Jews, but the Antioch church (Acts 13:1) consisted of Hellenistic Jews (Acts 11:19) and Greek-speaking Gentiles (Acts 11:20).[46] The situation in Jerusalem (Acts 6) is comparable to OBCs and LBCs who are separated by both language and a large cultural gap, while the situation in Antioch (Acts 11:19-21; 13:1) is similar to LBCs and people from the host culture who are separated by a relatively smaller cultural and no language gap. Therefore, the solution to the cultural conflict in Acts 6 supports the parallel ministry model for churches with OBCs and LBCs, and the multicultural situation in Acts 13:1 supports planting multicultural churches in areas where there are LBCs, but few or no OBCs.

The main practical strength of the separate service model is that it meets the needs of both OBCs and LBCs to a higher degree than the

---

[46] On the controversy over how to translate "'Ελληνιστής" in Acts 6:1; 9:29; 11:20, see the appendix: A Postscript on Multicultural Churches.

monolingual, bilingual, or church planting models do by providing worship to both groups in their own culture and language.[47]

One of the weakness of the separate service model is that since it views the church as a patriarchal hierarchy, then it only allows for a single senior pastor and board. This arrangement typically creates tension between the OBC senior pastor and LBC associate/assistant pastor in at least two ways. First, the LBC pastor is accountable to and required to follow the ministerial directions of a leader with whom they often cannot (effectively) communicate due to language and cultural differences and who frequently does not understand the needs of the LBC ministry. Second, there is normally the expectation that the OBC pastor will disciple the LBC pastor, but language and cultural differences as well as different visions and philosophies of ministry make such a discipleship relationship impractical and ineffective.

Additionally, since the single combined board of OBCs and LBCs makes all the decisions for both congregations, then several complications occur. Frist, there is typically a power struggle in the board over who will be the board chair. Second, there is also a power struggle involving the number of members from each congregation who will sit on the board. Separate service churches ordinarily attempt to address this concern by making board representation based on congregational size or by having equal numbers of board members regardless of congregational size. Both of these solutions ordinarily do not adequately resolve the tension. Third, there is the practical concern that the daily ministry decisions in each respective congregation are normally not relevant to the other congregation. Consequently, since OBCs typically control the board, LBCs need to sit through hours of irrelevant issues that OBCs could decide on their own and LBCs need to hold a separate meeting to address their immediate daily ministry concerns. Furthermore, LBCs are discouraged from serving on the board because they find it to be irrelevant and boring. If the board meeting is run in the OBC language, this situation further alienates LBCs. Fourth, when decisions such as church discipline arise, OBCs and LBCs practical application of the biblical instructions are often so culturally colored that board members cannot agree on the proper course of action.

Only the parallel ministry model effectively relieves these pastoral and board tensions by having co-pastors (Acts 6:2-6; 20:28; 1 Pet 5:2-4; Hebrews 13:20) and separate boards with equal authority (Acts 6:2-

---

[47] Chin, "Local–Born Chinese," 162.

4, 6). Decisively, the separate service model as presented by its proponents is really only a partial parallel ministry, because it does not sufficiently observe and apply all the elements of parallel ministry from Acts 6. Therefore, an Acts 6 full parallel ministry is needed to minimize the cycle of tension and avoid the inevitable consequences of the LBC exodus and church splits/plants.

Church Planting

In *Pursuing the Pearl*, Fong argues for the necessity of ministering to Americanized Asian Americans (AAAs, or third, fourth, fifth etc. generation Asians). Fong's argument seems to consist of three syllogistic-like claims:

1. AAAs are a homogeneous unit (chapters 1-4).
2. Acts 15 and 1 Corinthians 9:19-23 indicate that the Gospel should be contextualized for every homogeneous unit (chapter 5).
3. And since OBC churches cannot successfully contextualize the Gospel for AAAs, then new churches need to be planted to contextualize the Gospel for them (chapters 6-10).

The basis of Fong's ministry model is not biblical, but rather sociological. Fong explicitly admits that the term "homogeneous unit" is a sociological concept, and he borrows the definition from the "Lausanne Occasional Paper 13" of the Lausanne Committee on World Evangelization.[48] In defining the term "homogeneous unit," the "Lausanne Occasional Paper 13" is actually citing Dayton's definition of "people group," which, according to Starling, is an updated synonym for McGraven's original term of homogeneous unit: a "significantly large grouping of individuals who perceive themselves to have a common affinity for one another."[49] The concept "homogeneous unit" has been

---

48 Fong, Multi–Asian Ministry, 5–6.

49 Edward R. Dayton, *That Everyone May Hear: Reaching the Unreached*, 3rd ed. (Monrovia, CA: Missions Advanced Research and Communication Center, 1983), 18; Donald A. McGavran, *Understanding Church Growth*, ed. C. Peter Wagner (Grand Rapids: William B. Eerdmans, 1990), 69–70; Thailand Mini–Consultation on Reaching Muslims (1980: Ban Phatthaya, *The Thailand Report on Muslims: Report of the Consultation on World Evangelization Mini–Consultation on Reaching Muslims: Held*

hotly debated and criticized for being sociological rather than theological and even "directly opposed to the apostolic teaching" (Padilla) as part of a larger critique of the church growth movement and contemporary missiology.[50] The ecclesiological importance of the term homogeneous unit involves the debate over whether ministries should seek to intentionally serve groups of people who are similar (of one ethnicity/culture) or to intentinally serve "heterogeneous units," groups of people who are different or are made up of two or more different homogeneous units (multicultural minsitry). Furthermore, in arguing that AAAs are a homogeneous unit, Fong's chapters in defense of this claim are devoid of any biblical support for his assertion, and Fong explicitly admits that he is using sociology as interpreted by the church growth movement.[51] When Fong does refer to Scripture in the remainder of his book, his usage generally is consistent with Van Rheenen's criticism of the church growth movement: "Scripture is occasionally used, but only to give validity to some methodology or anthropological construct."[52]

However, in a later chapter, Fong claims that Acts 15:1-35 and 1 Corinthians 9:19-23 are the biblical basis of his argument that the Gospel should be "contextualized" for every homogeneous unit.[53] Even in

---

in Pattaya, Thailand from 16–27 June 1980 Lausanne Occasional Paper, vol. 13 (Wheaton, IL: Lausanne Committee for World Evangelization, 1980), 6; A. Starling, ed. *Seeds of Promise: World Consultation on Frontier Missions, Edinburgh '80,* International Bulletin of Missionary Research Book Awards; 1981 (Pasadena: W. Carey Library, 1981), 60.

[50] Bruce W. Fong, Racial Equality in the Church: A Critique of the Homogeneous Unit Principle in Light of a Practical Theology Perspective (Lanham, MD: University Press of America, 1996), 59–64, 85, 93–94; J. Robertson McQuilkin, Measuring the Church Growth Movement, Revised ed. (Chicago: Moody Press, 1974), 54–56; Jürgen Moltmann, The Gospel of Liberation, trans. H. Wayne Pipkin (Waco: Word Books, 1973), 91; René C. Padilla, "The Unity of the Church and the Homogeneous Unit Principle," in Exploring Church Growth, ed. Wilbert R. Shenk of International Bulletin of Missionary Research Book Awards (Grand Rapids: W.B. Eerdmans, 1983), 301; Gailyn Van Rheenen, "Reformist View: Church Growth Assumes Theology but Ineffectively Employs It to Analyze Culture, Determine Strategy, and Perceive History," in Evaluating the Church Growth Movement, ed. Paul E. Engle and Gary L. McIntosh, Zondervan Counterpoints Collection (Grand Rapids: Zondervan, 2004), in Logos Library System [CD–ROM], 176, 180.

[51] Fong, Multi–Asian Ministry, 5–6.

[52] Van Rheenen, "Reformist View," 175.

[53] Fong, *Multi–Asian Ministry*, 78, see also 77.

his attempt to provide a biblical basis for his argument, Fong mixes sociology and the Bible through the use of the term "contextualized." Fong only uses the term contextualization one time, but he refers to the concept repeatedly.[54] Contextualization is sometimes understood as "the communication of the Christian message from a home culture to a different one" by which the communicator will "tailor the gospel message to address different groups of people" in order to "overcome barriers [to understanding] inherent in the receiving cultures."[55] It is a sociological term originally put into use by liberal Christians to explain the process of preaching the Gospel in cross–cultural contexts.[56] According to Engle, the word "contextualization" was coined by Shoki Coe in 1972 as a technical term with regard to the field of missiology.[57] It is a hotly debated term and does not have a standard definition.[58] As debate over the term contextualization expands, the discussion has moved from missiology to other fields such as theology and biblical studies.[59] Part of the debate involves setting controls on contextualization in order to avoid two dangers inherent in the process: (1) mistaking one's own culture for the Gospel and (2) including elements of the receptor culture as part of the Gospel so that syncretism results.[60] (Syncretism is the combination of different, sometimes contradictory, beliefs or practices.) In order to recognize the other places Fong uses the concept of contextualization it is important to know that some synonyms for contextualization include: accommodation, adaptation, indigenization, incarnation, translation,

---

[54] Fong, *Multi–Asian Ministry*, 26; see also: 8, 35, 76-79, 83, 117, 138, 140, 143, 223.

[55] Dean E. Flemming, *Contextualization in the New Testament: Patterns for Theology and Mission* (Downers Grove: InterVarsity Press, 2005), 15, 19, 35; David J. Hesselgrave and Edward Rommen, *Contextualization: Meanings, Methods, and Models* (Pasadena: William Carey Library, 2000), 1.

[56] Richard W. Engle, "Contextualization in Missions: A Biblical and Theological Appraisal," *GTJ* 4, no. 1 (1983): 86, 100.

[57] Ibid., 87.

[58] George F. Peters, "Foreword," in *Contextualization: Meanings, Methods, and Models* (Pasadena: William Carey Library, 2000), ix.

[59] Flemming, Contextualization in the New Testament, 14.

[60] Hesselgrave and Rommen, *Contextualization*, 1.

transposition, and rereading of Scripture.[61] Flemming claims that inculturation is a related, but not a synonymous term.[62] Popularly, contextualization is thought of as trying to tailor the *delivery* (form) of the Gospel or theology to a particular culture, without compromising the *content* of the message. The classic example typically given is Paul's preaching in Athens where he claims that the Greek altar to the "unknown God" is an untintentional cultural reference to the God of the Bible (Acts 17:22–34).

Not only is Fong's use of contextualization sociological, but his appeal to Acts 15:1-35 and 1 Corinthians 9:19-23 as the biblical basis for his argument is also problematic. He states that these passages are the "assumption behind everything presented in this study thus far."[63] Fong argues that since the Jerusalem Council (Acts 15:1-35) and Paul (1 Corinthians 9:19-23) contextualized the Gospel for Gentiles, then the Gospel should be contextualized for AAAs.[64] Despite the fact that numerous proponents of contextualization appeal to Acts 15 as an example of contextualization, Wiarda has cogently argued that Acts 15 is not dealing with sociology (how to contextualize the Gospel for another culture), but rather theology/soteriology (that the basis of salvation is by grace through faith apart from works of the law such as circumcision, Acts 15:1, 11; Eph. 2:8–10).[65] Since the term contextualization was not coined until 1972 and its discussion did not move from missiology into biblical

---

[61] Flemming, Contextualization in the New Testament, 18.

[62] Ibid., 18.

[63] Fong, *Multi–Asian Ministry*, 78, see also 77.

[64] Ibid., 80.

[65] Timothy Wiarda, "The Jerusalem Council and the Theological Task," *JETS* 46, no. 2 (2003): 233–36, 245. In addition to Fong, other writers on the crisis of the immigrant church appeal to Acts 15: Rodriguez, *Latino Church*, K.l. 1433–38; Wong, "Culturally–Sensitive," 87–88; Wong, "American–Born Chinese," 33. Some proponents of contextualization who appeal to Acts 15 as an example include: John R. Davies, "Biblical Precedents for Contextualisation," *ATAJ* 2, no. 1 (1994): 21–22; Engle, "Contextualization in Missions," 96–97, 99; Flemming, *Contextualization in the New Testament*, 43–53; Hesselgrave and Rommen, *Contextualization*, 8–11; Charles H. Kraft, *Christianity in Culture: A Study in Dynamic Biblical Theologizing in Cross–Cultural Perspective* (Maryknoll, NY: Orbis, 1979), 34–35, 38, 287, 323, 340–41; David K. Strong, "The Jerusalem Council: Some Implications for Contextualization Acts 15:1–35," in *Mission in Acts: Ancient Narratives in Contemporary Context*, ed. Robert L. Gallagher and Paul Hertig, vol. 34 of American Society of Missiology (Maryknoll, NY: Orbis Books, 2004), 196–208.

studies until later, then older commentaries do not discuss contextualization. However, among the more recent commentators, Peterson explicitly sides with Wiarda in rejecting Acts 15 as an example of contextualization, Bock seems to side with Wiarda implicitly by explicitly naming Acts 14 and 17 as examples of contextualization, but omitting Acts 15, and Parsons argues that Acts 15 is an example of contextualization.[66] Consequently, there are good reasons to believe that Acts 15:1-35 does not even support the concept of contextualization.

Admittedly, there is more support for finding the concept of contextualization in 1 Corinthians 9:19-23 than in Acts 15:1-35. For example, Love reflects the fact that so many have appealed to 1 Corinthians 9:19-23 as the basis for contextualization that it may be called "the 'Magna Carta' of contextualization."[67] Despite the fact that in esteemed commentary series, scholars such as Chiampa and Thiselton, argue for contextualization in the passage, other renowned commentators, such as Fee and MacArthur, deny that contextualization is the point of 1 Corinthians 9:19-23.[68] Consequently, one stands in good company if they deny that 1 Corinthians 9:19-23 has to do with contextualization. However, even if one finds the concept of contextualization in some Bible passages, the notion itself is not enough to carry Fong's argument.

Even if one accepts that Fong's biblical support establishes the principle of contextualization for homogeneous units, it is a deficient basis

---

[66] Darrell L. Bock, *Acts*, BECNT (Grand Rapids: Baker Academic, 2007), in *Logos Library System* [CD–ROM], 17, 479, 558, 568; Mikeal C. Parsons, *Acts*, PCNT (Grand Rapids: Baker Academic, 2008), in *Logos Library System* [CD–ROM], 224; David G. Peterson, *The Acts of the Apostles*, PNTC (Grand Rapids: W.B. Eerdmans, 2009), in *Logos Library System* [CD–ROM], 443–45.

[67] Rick Love, Muslims, Magic and the Kingdom of God: Church Planting among Folk Muslims (Pasadena, CA: William Carey Library, 2000), 50.

[68] Roy E. Ciampa, and Brian S. Rosner, *The First Letter to the Corinthians*, PNTC (Grand Rapids: William B. Eerdmans, 2010), in *Logos Library System* [CD-ROM], 425; Gordon Fee, *The First Epistle to the Corinthians*, NICNT (Grand Rapids: William B. Eerdmans, 1988), in *Logos Library System* [CD-ROM], 432; John F. MacArthur, Jr., *Ashamed of the Gospel: When the Church Becomes Like the World*, 3rd ed. (Wheaton, IL: Crossway, 2010), 101-15, esp. 107; Anthony C. Thiselton, *The First Epistle to the Corinthians: A Commentary on the Greek Text*, NIGTC (Grand Rapids: W.B. Eerdmans, 2000), in *Logos Library System* [CD-ROM], 702-03.

for establishing church planting as a solution to the crisis of the immigrant church, because the process of contextualization does not necessitate church planting. In fact, Chin argues for the separate service model on the basis of the homogeneous unit principle, and Flemming (a proponent of contextualization) argues contrary to Fong that the contextualization in Acts 15 indicates that "homogeneous churches…must not be the dominant model for the people of God."[69]

Indeed, Fong's warrant for church planting is not really the principle of contextualizing the Gospel for homogeneous units (Acts 15; 1 Cor. 9), but rather his belief that since OBC churches cannot successfully contextualize the Gospel for AAAs, because they are too assimilated, then new churches need to be planted to contextualize the Gospel for them. For example, Fong claims, "First, a good number of first–generation churches will need to be convinced of the futility of the plans to reach saltwater generations…the third generation and beyond."[70] Fong's assumption is that in his spectrum of assimilation, there is an arbitrary break such that OBCs can reach the 1.5 and second generations, but not the "third generation and beyond" (AAAs), because they are too assimilated and can only be reached by LBC churches.[71] However, historically in at least three different types of ministries (para-church, separate service/partial parallel ministry services, and LBC churches including Ken Fong's church by his own admission), the LBCs from all generations have successfully interacted together in ministry.[72] This interaction implies that since LBCs throughout the spectrum of assimilation will relate together in the same ministry, then assimilation of different levels is not the problem. The problem is not a sociological *cannot*, but a biblical *have not;* OBCs have not been willing to implement parallel ministry by relinquishing financial and decision-making authority to LBCs, and LBCs have not been willing to risk the responsibilities of parallel ministry without the security of OBC financial support (Acts 6:1-7).

---

[69] Chin, "Local–Born Chinese," 162; Flemming, *Contextualization in the New Testament*, 53.

[70] Fong, *Multi–Asian Ministry*, 218, see also: 8–10, 194, 219.

[71] "Some will stay, especially the second–generation ones." Ibid., 25, 194, 218.

[72] Ibid., 1, 39, 73, 205–06; Russell Jeung, *Faithful Generations: Race and New Asian American Churches*, Kindle ed. (New Brunswick, NJ: Rutgers University Press, 2005), K.l. 576, 579–80; Phillips, "Haitian Church," 13; Jonathan Tran, "Why Asian American Christianity is the Future: Holding It Together in Yellow Christianity," *SANACS*, no. 2 (Sum 2010): 45.

Fong's proposal also breaks down, not only because it is really sociological rather than biblical, but also because it is based on invalid analogies drawn between both Acts 15 and 1 Corinthians 9:19-23 and with the crisis in the immigrant church.

In interpreting Acts 15, Fong misinterprets the soteriological (having to do with salvation) Jerusalem Council as a multicultural-sociological (homogeneous unit vs. heterogeneous ministry, contextualization) discussion, and then Fong incorrectly applies his multicultural-sociological interpretation to the ecclesiastical (church structure) aspect of the immigrant church crisis.[73] In Acts 15:11, the main point of the council is the basis of salvation as being of grace (vs. 11) rather than of the works of the law (vs. 5).[74] After the basis of salvation is established in Acts 15:11, Acts 15:20 addresses the issue of what spiritual and moral practices are consistent with Christian living or salvation by grace.[75] Whatever cultural tensions between Gentiles and Jews may underlie the soteriological discussion (any desire by Jews for Gentiles to assimilate to Jewish culture), these apply to the spiritual-relational rather than the ecclesiological aspect of the crisis of the immigrant church because Acts 15:20 does not prescribe a church structure or model, but rather addresses Christian living.[76]

Similarly, 1 Corinthians 9:19-23 deals with the spiritual-relational aspect of evangelism and missions rather than prescribing an ecclesiological structure or model for the church.[77] The passage primarily

---

[73] Fong, *Multi–Asian Ministry*, 77. Also see the discussion in: Bock, *Acts*, 487; Peterson, *Acts*, 421; John B. Polhill, *Acts*, NAC, vol. 26 (Nashville: Broadman & Holman, 1995), in *Logos Library System* [CD–ROM], 321.

[74] Bock, *Acts*, 487; F. F. Bruce, *The Book of Acts*, Revised ed., NICNT (Grand Rapids: William B. Eerdmans, 1988), 282; Craig S. Keener, *Acts: An Exegetical Commentary*, Kindle ed., vol. 3 (Grand Rapids: Baker Academic, 2014); K.l. 3842–43, 4278–81.

[75] Bruce, *Acts*, 282.

[76] Keener, *Acts*, K.l. 3:4344–45, 4647, 4652–53.

[77] Ciampa and Rosner, *Corinthians*, 425–26, 430; Gordon Fee, *The First Epistle to the Corinthians*, NICNT (Grand Rapids: William B. Eerdmans, 1988), in *Logos Library System* [CD–ROM]), 432; Alan F. Johnson, *1 Corinthians*, vol. 7, The IVP New Testament Commentary Series (Downers Grove, IL: InterVarsity, 2004), in *Logos Library System* [CD–ROM], 147–49; Thiselton, *Corinthian*, 702–03.

is concerned with one's attitude and associated practices toward other cultures in the act of preaching the Gospel to them through how one lives. The context of this preaching is the specific issue of Christian living of whether or not one should eat meat sacrificed to idols.

Furthermore, the multicultural principles inferred from the respective passages by Fong of not imposing one's culture on others (multiculturalism's cultural imperialism; Acts 15) and adapting various ministry methods to different cultures (multiculturalism's celebration of diversity; 1 Cor. 9:19-23) do not necessitate the church planting model and may be reasonably implemented in the separate service, parallel ministry models, and perhaps to a lesser extent, in the bilingual ministry model. This is not to say that a church should implement the principles of multiculturalism, none should, but rather that these principles in and of themselves do not necessitate Fong's model and are not consist with Scripture. Therefore, while Acts 15:1-35 and 1 Corinthians 9:19-23 may have some applicability to the spiritual-relational aspect of the immigrant church crisis, they are invalid analogies to the ecclesiastical aspect, because they are not dealing with the issue of church structure in relation to cultural tensions. In other words, these passages are instructions on what attitudes to have toward one another in the midst of a cultural conflict, but they do not explain how to structure the church to resolve it.

The greatest strength of the church planting model is also its greatest weakness: it more adequately meets the needs of *some* LBCs more than the bilingual and separate service models. Although church planting proponents claim that their target group is unchurched LBCs, they also recognize that their church plants have "indirectly helped expedite, the Silent Exodus" (Tran) by also attracting 1.5 and second generation LBCs from OBC churches.[78] Consequently, if the separate worship service model raises OBC concerns about dividing families, then the church planting model realizes these concerns.[79]

When LBCs leave an OBC church and join an LBC church, their needs are more adequately met, but the OBCs have a harder time

---

[78] Eng, "Overview," 70–71; Fong, *Multi–Asian Ministry*, 1, 39, 73, 205–06; Jeung, *Faithful Generations*, K.l. 1259–60; Helen Lee, "Silent Exodus: Can the East Asian Church in America Reverse the Flight of Its Next Generation?," *Christianity Today* 40, no. 9 (1996): 53; Phillips, "Haitian Church," 13; Jonathan Tran, "Why Asian American Christianity Has No Future: The over against, Leaving Behind, and Separation from of Asian American Christian Identity," *SANACS*, no. 2 (Sum 2010): 25.

[79] Wong, "Future Need," 172.

meeting their own needs and the needs of the remaining LBCs who do not leave. As a result of the LBC exodus, the OBC church loses financial and staffing resources (both volunteer and professional) as well as role models to run the ministry for the remaining LBCs.[80] Furthermore, some OBC parents who would be the biggest supporters of LBC ministry if they stayed in an OBC church, also leave for LBC churches in order to make sure their children's needs are met and for other reasons.[81] Additionally, when the OBCs get older, they do not have the support of their children to maintain their ministry, and those LBCs who later have children may decide they want to go back to an OBC church, either for their children to be with their grandparents or in order for their children to get in touch with their roots, have no viable church to which to return.[82]

For these reasons, the church planting model is actually a counterproductive solution to the crisis of the immigrant church. Furthermore, while church planting for other reasons is certainly biblical, church planting designed to resolve the crisis of the immigrant church is not only counterproductive, but also contradicts Acts 6:1–7 which indicates that the cultural crisis is to be resolved by maintaining one church through parallel ministry. However, LBC church plants might be able to overcome these weaknesses by partnering with OBC ministries, as some church planters propose and as some LBC church plants have actually done, but such a solution really only approximates and points to the need for the parallel ministry model proposed by this book.[83]

At this point, many readers may expect to see case studies to demonstrate that these past proposals have historically been deficient in practice. Historically, the very few surviving hundred to two hundred year old immigrant founded chuches in the United States and the contining occurrence of the crisis are sufficient evidence to indicate the historical

---

[80] Young Lee Hertig, "Reflections on the Inaugural Asian American Equipping Symposium," *SANACS*, no. 2 (Sum 2010): 9; Phillips, "Haitian Church," 173; Wong, "Future Need," 172–73.

[81] Phillips, "Haitian Church," 13; Rodriguez, *Latino Church*, K.l. 930–32.

[82] Jeung, *Faithful Generations*, K.l. 576, 579–80; Phillips, "Haitian Church," 174.

[83] Fong, *Multi–Asian Ministry*, 193; Jeung, *Faithful Generations*, K.l. 1115–16; Rodriguez, *Latino Church*, K.l. 986–87.

deficiency of the past proposals. Even though the historical failure of the past proposals is undeniable and is evidence in favor of the need for the current proposal for parallel ministry, the validity of the present argument ultimately does not depend on the pragmatic failure of the other proposals. Instead, the current proposal rests on its own biblical consistency and the biblical inconsistency of the other proposals.

If readers would like to see case studies, then the *FACE Handbook*, Fong, Jeung, and the other sociologically based works cited throughout this book provide ample sociological studies of ineffective minsitries and ministries that appear to be effecive, but are really under the "illusion of success," all of which are forms of the three past proposals (bilingual, separate service, and church planting). Since the bilingual, separate service, and church planting models are deficient, then another model is needed to solve the crisis of the immigrant church. The parallel ministry model described in chapters 2 and 3 is the only biblically based model that adequately addresses the concerns and needs of both OBCs and LBCs described in chapter 1 and solves the crisis of the immigrant church.

CONCLUSION

Depending on which statistics are followed, anywhere from 75-90% of LBCs historically are lost from each generation of OBC churches every year in North America.[1] In *Dying for Change*, Leith Anderson addresses this type of situation in churches by stating that:

---

[1] Moses Chow and David T. Chow, "Practical Cooperation Programs and Projects between Overseas–Born Chinese and Local–Born Chinese," in *ECCWE*, ed. Sharon Wai–Man Chan (Tsim Sha Tsui, Hong Kong: Chinese Coordination Centre of World Evangelism, 1986), 152; Joseph C. Wong, "Culturally–Sensitive OBC Leadership," in *FACE* (Oakland, CA: Fellowship of American Chinese Evangelicals (FACE), 2009), 78. In contrast, Kinnaman and Aly Hawkins and Schultz and Joani Schultz place the general dropout rate in all U.S. churches at 43%. David Kinnaman and Aly Hawkins, *You Lost Me: Why Young Christians Are Leaving Church...And Rethinking Faith* (Grand Rapids: Baker, 2011), 22; Thom Schultz and Joani Schultz, *Why Nobody Wants to Go to Church Anymore: And How 4 Acts of Love Will Make Your Church Irresistible*, Kindle ed. (Loveland, CO: Group, 2013), K.l. 243. Dyck has 70–80% for the host culture, but Shields disputes this figure and places it at 7%–22%. Consequently, the 43% number that has some consensus seems reasonably conservative being between 70%–80%. Drew Dyck, *Generation Ex–Christian: Why Young Adults Are Leaving the Faith...And How to Bring Them Back*, Revised ed. (Chicago: Moody, 2010), 17; Brandon Shields, "Family–Based Ministry: Shared Contexts, Shared Focus," in *Perspectives on Family Ministry: Three Views*, ed. Timothy Paul Jones (Nashville, TN: B&H, 2009), 102–06. Barna claims that the dropout rate between whites and Asians is about the same, but his statistics seem to be for dropouts from host culture churches and not immigrant churches. George Barna and David Kinnaman, eds., *Churchless: Understanding Today's Unchurched and How to Connect with Them* (Carol Stream, IL: Tyndale, 2014), 38–39. If one takes the 43% and 75–90% figures, then due to the cultural tensions LBCs face with OBCs on top of

> Many of the sincere and committed Christians who still faithfully fill the family pews in these churches hold on to the nostalgic hope that tomorrow will be yesterday. Others desperately want their churches to catch up with the times and meet the challenges of the present generation, but they don't know how. And still others … fight the inevitable changes for the sake of traditions that would be better abandoned. … Change is an unavoidable part of life. … Sometimes we react so strongly against the changes we dislike that we either try to ignore them or use all our resources to reverse them. … Change is not the choice. How we handle it is.[2]

Returning to the hypothetical pastor of the First Church of the Immigrant Believer we met in the introduction, he chose to handle the changes facing his congregation by moving in the direction of parallel ministry. He hired an LBC co-pastor to form, lead, and raise up leaders from an LBC interdependent and parallel congregation.

> The church formed a first-rate search committee to find just the right LBC pastor by promoting in their internet job description that they were looking to form an interdependent parallel ministry. The man they finally found was young but experienced, serious but witty, articulate but not intimidating, spiritual but world-wise. If anyone could help them overcome the crisis of their immigrant church, he was the man. When the pastoral candidate first addressed the church during a joint service, he gave an inspiring description of his qualifications, experience, vision, and plans. His final line summed up his stirring presentation: "With God's help, I intend to lead this church forward into the twentieth century!" Surprised and embarrassed by the candidate's apparent mistake, an LBC member whispered loudly, "You mean the twenty-first century." To which the candidate replied, "We're going to take this one century at a time!"[3]

Change can be slow and painful requiring many precious sacrifices. However, in the case of the crisis of the immigrant church, the Bible points the way. Acts 6:1-7 explicitly resolves the crisis of the immigrant church by transferring financial and decision-making authority to the next generation so that they can create a culturally relevant parallel ministry that allows for everyone's needs to be met in the church, both OBC and LBC. In light of this situation, all immigrant churches essentially are facing two choices: change or close their doors with the older generation. This is because an unwillingness on the part of OBCs to change to accommodate the needs of the next generations, results in the

---

the typical faith and host culture struggles, the LBC dropout rate is around double their host culture counterparts.

[2] Leith Anderson, *Dying for Change* Kindle ed. (Minneapolis: Bethany House Publishers, 1990), K.l. 36–39, 42, 44–45, 50.

[3] Adapted from: ibid., 30–35.

fact that most LBCs will be lost. If a choice is not made to change, then the church will experience the illusion of success as OBC immigrants continue to flow into the church from overseas and LBCs silently disappear from the pews generation after generation. In addition, when immigration stops, the OBC congregation will eventually come to recognize the illusion of success, but then it will be too late as all the LBCs will be gone, and the church will eventually close its doors with the OBCs. If not that, then some small remnant of LBCs remain when immigration stops, but when the OBC generation fades into the night, that remnant will be less spiritually mature and much smaller numerically than if they had benefited from parallel ministry. If the church chooses to change and implement Acts 6, then a spiritual environment will be created from which both OBCs and LBCs will mutually benefit.

Act wisely, but quickly, remembering that the seven-year critical window of opportunity for reaching the LBC youth in your church is rapidly closing. Acts 6, parallel ministry must be implemented not only to stop the silent exodus so that LBCs will not fall away and not only to preserve immigrant churches and not only to prevent OBC hearts from breaking, but also so that both OBCs and LBCs may reach spiritual maturity and unity (Eph. 4:2-6, 13, 16). Change is not the choice. How we handle it is. What will you do?

APPENDIX:
A Postscript on Multicultural Churches

It is the contention of this book that the solution of parallel ministry (Acts 6:1-7) only applies to immigrant churches or churches that fit the description of being multi-lingual, multi-congregational and does not apply to mono-lingual, multiethnic churches (Acts 11:19-20; 13:1; see "Table 4: Multiethnic Church Models" at the end of this appendix).[1] Ortiz claims that a multi-congregational church has one facility for different groups, congregations that are separated by language, and congregations that usually have little inter-involvement together.[2] It is debated whether these types of churches can be considered multiethnic churches. Similarly, Ortiz defines a multiethnic church as being both quantitative and qualitative in that it has a "significantly" diverse membership utilizing one language and in which no one majority controls the "tradition" and "power structure" of the church.[3] A major purpose of a multi-ethnic church is reconciliation. Just as in the discussion of multi-lingual, multi-congregational churches or immigrant churches, Acts 6:1-7 has been the focus of much of the literature, so in the discussion of the multicultural or multiethnic church, Acts 11 and 13 are repeatedly mentioned.[4]

---

[1] These terms are borrowed from Ortiz: Manuel Ortiz, *One New People: Models for Developing a Multiethnic Church*, Kindle ed. (Downers Grove: InterVarsity, 1996), K.l. 510–14, 717–62.

[2] Ibid., K.l. 510–14.

[3] Ibid., K.l. 717–62.

[4] With regard to Acts 6:1–7 see: Mercidieu Phillips, "Resolving the Causes of Second Generation Exodus from the Haitian Church in South Florida" (D.Ed.Min. diss., Bethel Seminary, Saint Paul, MN, 2011), 31–32; Daniel A. Rodriguez, *A Future for the Latino Church: Models for Multilingual, Multigenerational Hispanic Congregations*, Kindle ed. (IVP Academic, 2011), K.l. 97–136; Joseph C. Wong, "The Biblical Basis for Promoting Effective ABC Ministries," in *FACE* (Oakland, CA: FACE, 2009), 19–20. With regad to Acts 11; 13 see: Ken Davis, "Multicultural Church Planting Models," *JMT* (Spring 2003): 115; Mark DeYmaz, *Building a Healthy Multi–Ethnic Church: Mandate, Commitments and Practices of a Diverse Congregation*, Kindle ed. (San Francisco: Jossey–Bass, 2007), K.l. 2, 19, 23; Ortiz, *Multiethnic Church*, K.l. 444; George A. Yancey, *One Body, One Spirit: Principles of Successful Multiracial Churches*, Kindle ed. (Downers Grove: InterVarsity, 2003), K.l. 49–50.

While this division of passages may not have been intentional, it is not arbitrary as "Antioch, not Jerusalem, was the model of the 'new church' which was to appear all over the world. It was founded by Hellenist Jews," not Hebraic Jews.[5] Consequently, authors unintentionally segregate Acts 6 and the passages in Acts 11 and 13 in the discussions of ecclesiastical structures because these two sets of passages present two different models of churches that are biblical examples or solutions to two different church problems or settings. By definition, Acts 6 addresses the situation of multi-lingual, multi-congregational churches experiencing cultural conflict and the passages in Acts 11 and 13 addresses the situation of mono-lingual multiethnic churches.

The contemporary church has erred by applying Acts 6 to the multiethnic church and the passages in Acts 11 and 13 to the multi-lingual, multi-congregational or immigrant church. Readers investigating this book for a solution to the crisis of multiethnic ministry should not attempt to apply Acts 6 to their church setting, as the model of Acts 11 and 13 is the relevant analogy or biblical example/solution to their problem.

By definition, Acts 6:1-7 deals with and so only applies to multi-lingual, multi-congregational or immigrant churches experiencing cultural conflict. Chapters 2 and 3 demonstrated that in Acts 6:1 the Hebraic and Hellenistic Jewish Christians represent two cultural-linguistic groups that were having a cultural conflict.[6] These two groups were of the same ethnicity, Jewish, and differed in language (Hebraists speaking

---

[5] D. W. B. Robinson, "Church," in *New Bible Dictionary*, ed. D. R. W. Wood and I. Howard Marshall (Downers Grove: InterVarsity, 1996), in *Logos Library System* [CD–ROM], 201.

[6] Darrell L. Bock, *Acts*, BECNT (Grand Rapids: Baker Academic, 2007), in *Logos Library System* [CD–ROM], 258; Craig S. Keener, *Acts: An Exegetical Commentary*, Kindle ed., vol. 2 (Grand Rapids: Baker Academic, 2013), K.l. 8537–41, 8574, 8579–80, 8628, 8630–32, 8657–58, 8661–62; Ricahrd N. Longenecker, *The Acts of the Apostles*, ed. Frank E. Gaebelein and J. D. Douglas, in vol. 9 of *EBC* (Grand Rapids: Zondervan, Regency Reference Library, 1981), in *QuickVerse* [CD–ROM], (Grand Rapids, MI: The Zondervan Corporation, 1976), 329, 332; Mikeal C. Parsons, *Acts*, PCNT (Grand Rapids: Baker Academic, 2008), in *Logos Library System* [CD-ROM], 82; John B. Polhill, *Acts*, NAC, vol. 26 (Nashville: Broadman & Holman, 1995), in *Logos Library System* [CD–ROM], 178–79; Ben Witherington, III, *The Acts of the Apostles: A Socio–Rhetorical Commentary* (Grand Rapids: W. B. Eerdmans, 1998), in *Logos Library System* [CD–ROM], 240–42, 250.

Aramaic and Hellenists Greek) and in culture (the Hellenists being more Hellenized or acculturated to the dominant Greco-Roman host culture than the Hebraists). Although they met in different house churches to worship in their own languages, they were part of one church, the Jerusalem church (Acts 6:7; 8:1; 11:22).[7] Therefore, Acts 6:1-7 is describing a multi-lingual, multi-congregational or immigrant church because there were two cultural-linguistic groups meeting separately in one place.

By definition, Acts 11:19-21 and Acts 13:1 deal with and so only apply to mono-lingual, multiethnic churches. In Acts 11:19, some of the Hellenists from the Jerusalem church who were scattered as a result of the persecution in connection with Stephen in Acts 6:8-8:1 shared their faith only with Jews. However, in Acts 11:20, some of these Hellenistic Jewish Christians from the Jerusalem church shared their faith with "Ἑλληνιστής" (Greek-speaking Gentiles), and as a result, the church at Antioch was formed (Acts 11:26).[8] Unlike the Jerusalem church in which there was a division due to language (Aramaic speaking Hebraists and Greek speaking Hellenists), at Antioch, the term "Ἑλληνιστής" in Acts 11:20 indicates that the church was mono-lingual, speaking Greek as their common language.[9] Furthermore, it is commonly recognized that, in Acts

---

[7] F. F. Bruce, *The Book of Acts*, Revised ed., NICNT (Grand Rapids: William B. Eerdmans, 1988), 120, 261; Keener, *Acts 3:1–14:28*, K.l. 2:9634–59, 9684–86; I. Howard Marshall, *The Acts of the Apostles: An Introduction and Commentary*, Reprint ed., TNTC, vol. 5 (Grand Rapids: William B. Eerdmans, 1989), 126; R. P. Martin, "Worship and Liturgy," in *Dictionary of the Later New Testament and Its Developments*, ed. Ralph P. Martin and Peter H. Davids (Downers Grove: InterVarsity, 1997), in *Logos Library System* [CD–ROM], s. v. "5. The Rome–Asia Minor Axis;" Longenecker, *Acts*, 329; David G. Peterson, *The Acts of the Apostles*, PNTC (Grand Rapids: W.B. Eerdmans, 2009), in *Logos Library System* [CD–ROM], 239–40; Polhill, *Acts*, 179, 184; Rainer Reisner, "Synagogues in Jerusalem," in *BAPS*, ed. Richard Bauckham, vol. 4 of The Book of Acts in Its First Century Setting (Grand Rapids: William B. Eerdmans 1995), 188–89, 192–200, 204–06; Emil Schürer, "Alexandrians in Jerusalem," in *The Jewish Encyclopedia*, ed. Isidore Singer (New York: Funk & Wagnalls, 1906), 371–72; Stanley D. Toussaint, "Acts," in *BKC*, ed. John F. Walvoord and Roy B. Zuck (Wheaton, IL: Victor Books, 1985), in *Logos Library System* [CD–ROM], 2:367; R. S. Wallace, "Lord's Supper (Eucharist)," in *ISBE*, ed. Geoffrey W. Bromiley (Grand Rapids: Wm. B. Eerdmans, 1988), in *Logos Library System* [CD–ROM], 3:167.

[8] On the debate over the meaning of the term "Ἑλληνιστής" in Acts see: Bock, *Acts*, 414; Peterson, *Acts*, 352–53; Bruce Manning Metzger, *A Textual Commentary on the Greek New Testament*, 2nd ed. (New York: United Bible Societies, 1994), in *Logos Library System* [CD–ROM], 340–42; Witherington, *Acts*, 242.

[9] Peterson, *Acts*, 352.

13:1, the list of names and locations indicates that the Antioch church was multicthnic with Hellenistic Jews and Gentiles from various locations.[10] Acts 13:2 demonstrates that these multiethnic church leaders were worshipping together.[11] Therefore, Acts 11:19-21 and Acts 13:1 describe the church at Antioch as being a mono-lingual, multiethnic church, which met as one congregation to worship (Acts 13:2) in a common language (Acts 11:20) with multiethnic leadership (Acts 13:1).

Therefore, Acts 6 and the passages in Acts 11 and 13 describe two different church models to deal with two different types of church settings or problems. When there are different cultural groups of the same ethnicity who are divided by language and are experiencing cultural conflict, then the parallel ministry structure of Acts 6 with interdependent leadership and separate worship in different languages applies. When there are different ethnic groups who speak the same language, then as in Acts 11:20 and in 13:1-2, they worship together in language in the same location and have an ethnically diverse leadership team. For example, Sullivan's study describes a common multicultural situation in contemporary America in which immigrants from Asia, the Middle East, Mexico, South-Central America, and the Caribbean all meet in parallel congregations at Catherine's Catholic Church and in which the LBCs of each congregation feel that their needs are unmet by the OBCs in their respective congregations.[12] According to Acts 6 and the situation described in Acts 11 and 13, these different ethnic immigrant groups should not worship in parallel meetings like in Acts 6, but rather should either meet as separate churches with parallel ministries for each ethnicity's OBCs and LBCs (Acts 6) or decide for all the OBCs to worship

---

[10] Bock, *Acts*, 438–39; Mikeal C. Parsons, *Acts*, PCNT (Grand Rapids: Baker Academic, 2008), in *Logos Library System* [CD–ROM], 184; Peterson, *Acts*, 374; Polhill, *Acts*, 289; Toussaint, "Acts," 2:387.

[11] There is some debate as to whether the verse depicts the entire congregation worshipping together or just the leaders, but presumably if the leaders worshipped together then so did the congregation. Bock, *Acts*, 438–39; Parsons, *Acts*, 184; Peterson, *Acts*, 375; Polhill, *Acts*, 290.

[12] Kathleen Sullivan, "Catherine's Catholic Church: One Church, Parallel Congregations," in *Religion and the New Immigrants: Continuities and Adaptations*, Kindle ed., Helen Rose Ebaugh and Janet Saltzman Chafetz, eds. (Walnut Creek, CA: Altamira Press, 2000), pp. 255–90.

together in one congregation by using the common language of the host culture, English in this case (Acts 11:20; 13:1-2), and have all the LBC's meet in a parallel ministry (Acts 6).

Additionally, LBCs of various levels of assimilation, whether of the same or different ethnicities, should not worship in parallel meetings as in Acts 6, because typically, they all speak the host language and are able to worship together despite their cultural differences, like the Hellenistic Jews and Gentiles did in Acts 11:20 and in Acts 13:1-2. The solution of parallel ministry (Acts 6:1-7) only applies to immigrant churches or churches that fit the description of being multi-lingual, multi-congregational and does not apply to mono-lingual, multiethnic churches (Acts 11:19-20; 13:1).

Table 4: Multiethnic Church Models

Multi-Lingual Multi-Congregational			**Mono-Lingual Multiethnic**	
Definitions				
A multi-congregational church has one facility, for different groups, that are separated by language, and usually have little inter-involvement together. It is debatable if these are truly MEC's.			A multiethnic church is both quantitative and qualitative: it has a "significantly" diverse membership utilizing one language and in which no one majority controls the "tradition" and "power structure" of the church. A major purpose of the church is reconciliation.	
Models/Description				
	Renting	Celebrating	Integrating	Mono-Congregational
Motivation	"The 'landlord' church rents the facilities as a ministry to its community, which has undergone ethnic transition."	"The inviting church would like to have more of a relationship with other groups and would like to see growth in the congregation through encouraging the second generation of the other congregations to attend its services."	The church Is concerned with diversity but may or may not be concerned with reconciliation and social justice (The examples below are concerned with both.).	Concerned not only with diversity but ethnic reconciliation with social justice in ministry (change of power structure in the church).
Characteristics	Relationships are usually superficial. A problem typically begins with disagreement on building maintenance. Characterized by mutual exploitation: the 'landlord' experiences superficial growth and the 'renter' gets a facility.	Joint services on the major holidays & church anniversaries. Inviting church usually has no intention of "sharing the ownership" (of the property or decision making power). Inviting church does evangelism but wants to preserve its cultural and church tradition.	Congregations may mutually own the property and decision making power. The main divisions between the congregations are language and culture. (May include the single service "parallel translation" model in here as well.)	Has a diversity of ethnicities meeting as one congregation using a common language which in our country is usually English.
Multiethnic Dynamic	Essentially a business relationship with physical but no relational closeness.	"Assimilationist" - "invites people of diversity to join the group as long as they conform to the dominant group."	"Integration" – "The integrative model seeks integration of the various ethnic groups. It allows the diversity presented by the various groups, but the group's operating format [may be] governed by a dominant group."	"Involvement" – "does not represent the various ethnic groups but involves all the different [identifiable] ethnicities in establishing and forming the [ministry]."
Examples	Some immigrant churches likely fit this model.	Some LBC congregations may fit this model.	First Church of the Nazarene in downtown Los Angeles. First Baptist Church in Flushing, New York.	International Bible Church in Los Angeles, CA Rock of Our Salvation in Chicago, Illinois

Source: Manuel Ortiz, *One New People: Models for Developing a Multiethnic Church*, Kindle ed. (Downers Grove: InterVarsity, 1996), K.l. 330-466, 510-14, 717-62.

BIBLIOGRAPHY

Anderson, Leith. *Dying for Change* Kindle ed. Minneapolis: Bethany House Publishers, 1990.

Barna, George, and David Kinnaman, eds. *Churchless: Understanding Today's Unchurched and How to Connect with Them*. Carol Stream, IL: Tyndale, 2014.

Bauckham, Richard. "James and the Jerusalem Church." In *The Book of Acts in Its Palestinian Setting*, ed. Richard Bauckham, 415–80. Vol. 4 of The Book of Acts in Its First Century Setting. Grand Rapids: William B. Eerdmans 1995.

Bayor, Ronald H. "Series Foreword." In *The Chinese Americans*. The New Americans. Ed. Ronald H. Bayor. Westport, CT: Greenwood, 2000.

Benson, Robert J., Pieter M. Ribbers, and Ronald B. Blitstein. *Trust and Partnership: Strategic IT Management for Turbulent Times*. Wiley CIO Series. Hoboken, NJ: Wiley, 2014.

Bergé, Jean-Michel, Oz Levia, and Jacques Rouillard, eds. *Hardware/Software Co-Design and Co-Verification*. Current Issues in Electronic Modeling, vol. 8. Boston: Kluwer, 1997.

Bhushan, Vidya, and D. R. Sachdeva. *Fundamentals of Sociology*. Delhi, India: Pearson, 2012.

Bock, Darrell L. *Acts*. Baker Exegetical Commentary on the New Testament. Grand Rapids: Baker Academic, 2007. In *Logos Library System* [CD-ROM].

Bonsirven, Joseph. *Palestinian Judaism in the Time of Jesus Christ*. New York: Holt, Rinehart & Winston, 1964.

Brant, Jo-Ann. "The Place of Mimēsis in Paul's Thought." *Studies in Religion/Sciences religieuses* 22, no. 3 (1993): 285–300.

Breshears, Clay. *The Art of Concurrency: A Thread Monkey's Guide to Writing Parallel Applications*. Beijing: O'Reilly, 2009.

Bromiley, G. W. "Church." In *The International Standard Bible Encyclopedia*, ed. Geoffrey W. Bromiley, 1:693–96. Grand Rapids: Wm. B. Eerdmans, 1988. In *Logos Library System* [CD-ROM].

Bruce, F. F. *The Book of Acts*. The New International Commentary on the New Testament. Revised ed. Grand Rapids: William B. Eerdmans, 1988.

Cairns, Alan. *Dictionary of Theological Terms*. Greenville, SC: Ambassador Emerald International, 2002. In *Logos Library System* [CD-ROM].

Chan, Cecilia C. "Where Have the Children Gone?: Young Adult Commitment in Chinese Protestant Churches in United States." D.M. diss., Case Western Reserve University, Cleveland, OH, 2007.

Chan, David K. "Church Planting in Multi-Cultural Situation." In *Ethnic Chinese Congress on World Evangelization*, ed. Sharon Wai-Man Chan, 173–76. Tsim Sha Tsui, Hong Kong: Chinese Coordination Centre of World Evangelism, 1986.

________. "Practical Ways of Increasing Understanding between Overseas-Born Chinese and Local-Born Chinese." In *Ethnic Chinese Congress on World Evangelization*, ed. Sharon Wai-Man Chan, 143–44. Tsim Sha Tsui, Hong Kong: Chinese Coordination Centre of World Evangelism, 1986.

Chan, Ernest. "Appreciating Cultural Distinctives of the Local-Born Chinese." In *Ethnic Chinese Congress on World Evangelization*, ed. Sharon Wai-Man Chan, 107–08. Tsim Sha Tsui, Hong Kong: Chinese Coordination Centre of World Evangelism, 1986.

Chan, Sharon Wai-Man, ed. *Ethnic Chinese Congress on World Evangelization.* Tsim Sha Tsui, Hong Kong: Chinese Coordination Centre of World Evangelism, 1986.

Chan, Sucheng. *Asian Americans: An Interpretive History*. Twayne's Immigrant Heritage of America, Edited by Thomas J. Archdeacon. Revised and Updated ed. Boston: Twayne, 1991.

Capper, Brian. "The Palestinian Cultural Context of Earliest Christian Community of Goods." In *The Book of Acts in Its Palestinian Setting*, ed. Richard Bauckham, 323–56. Vol. 4 of *Book of Acts in Its First Century Setting*. Grand Rapids: William B. Eerdmans 1995.

Carlson, Kenneth P. "Patterns in Development of the English Ministry in a Chinese Church." In *The 2008 Report: The Bay Area Chinese Churches Research Project Phase II*, ed. James Chuck and Timothy Tseng, 207–12. Castro Valley, CA: The Institute for the Study of Asian American Christianity, 2009.

Cheung, Fred. "Bridging Racial and Linguistic Gaps." In *Ethnic Chinese Congress on World Evangelization*, ed. Sharon Wai-Man Chan, 65–68. Tsim Sha Tsui, Hong Kong: Chinese Coordination Centre of World Evangelism, 1986.

Chin, Steven J. "Reaching and Discipling Local-Born Chinese." In *Ethnic Chinese Congress on World Evangelization*, ed. Sharon Wai-Man Chan, 162–64. Tsim Sha Tsui, Hong Kong: Chinese Coordination Centre of World Evangelism, 1986.

Ciampa, Roy E., and Brian S. Rosner. *The First Letter to the Corinthians*. The Pillar New Testament Commentary. Grand Rapids: William B. Eerdmans, 2010. In *Logos Library System* [CD-ROM].

Chow, Moses, and David T. Chow. "Practical Cooperation Programs and Projects between Overseas-Born Chinese and Local-Born Chinese." In *Ethnic Chinese Congress on World Evangelization*, ed. Sharon Wai-Man Chan, 150–52. Tsim Sha Tsui, Hong Kong: Chinese Coordination Centre of World Evangelism, 1986.

Cladis, George. *Leading the Team-Based Church: How Pastors and Church Staffs Can Grow Together into a Powerful Fellowship of*

Leaders. San Francisco: Jossey-Bass, 1999.

Cox, D. Michael, and Brad J. Kallenberg. "Character." In *Dictionary of Scripture and Ethics*, Kindle ed., Joel B. Green, ed., K.l. 5728–5868. Grand Rapids: Baker Academic, 2011.

Davies, John R. "Biblical Precedents for Contextualisation." *Asia Theological Association Journal* 2, no. 1 (1994): 10–35.

Davis, Ken. "Multicultural Church Planting Models." *The Journal of Ministry & Theology* (Spring 2003): 114–27.

Dayton, Edward R. *That Everyone May Hear: Reaching the Unreached*. 3rd ed. Monrovia, CA: Missions Advanced Research and Communication Center, 1983.

DeYmaz, Mark. *Building a Healthy Multi-Ethnic Church: Mandate, Commitments and Practices of a Diverse Congregation*. Kindle ed. San Francisco: Jossey-Bass, 2007.

Doucet, Fabienne, and Carola Suarez-Orozco. "Ethnic Identity and Schooling the Experiences of Haitian Immigrant Youth." In *Ethnic Identity: Problems and Prospects for the Twenty-First Century*, 4th, Kindle ed., Lola Romanucci-Ross, De George A. Vos and Takeyuki Tsuda, eds. K.l. 3407–3920. New York: Alta Mira Press, 2006.

Dunn, James D. G. *The Epistle to the Galatians*. Black's New Testament Commentary. London: Continuum, 1993. In *Logos Library System* [CD-ROM].

Dyck, Drew. *Generation Ex-Christian: Why Young Adults Are Leaving the Faith...And How to Bring Them Back*. Revised ed. Chicago: Moody, 2010.

Edersheim, Alfred. *The Life and Times of Jesus the Messiah*. 8th, Revised ed. New York: Longmans, Green, and Co., 1962.

Ellingworth, Paul. *The Epistle to the Hebrews: A Commentary on the*

Greek Text. New International Greek Testament Commentary Grand Rapids: W.B. Eerdmans, 1993. In *Logos Library System* [CD-ROM].

Eng, William L. "Church Programs That Minister Effectively to ABCs." In *Completing the Face of the Chinese Church in America: The ABC Handbook Promoting Effective Ministries to American-Born Chinese*, 129–50. Oakland, CA: Fellowship of American Chinese Evangelicals (FACE), 2009.

________. "Having an Effective Model for ABC Ministry within the Chinese Church." In *Completing the Face of the Chinese Church in America: The ABC Handbook Promoting Effective Ministries to American-Born Chinese*, 101–19. Oakland, CA: Fellowship of American Chinese Evangelicals (FACE), 2009.

________. "An Overview of Christian Work among ABCs." In *Completing the Face of the Chinese Church in America: The ABC Handbook Promoting Effective Ministries to American-Born Chinese*, 51–73. Oakland, CA: Fellowship of American Chinese Evangelicals (FACE), 2009.

Eng, William L., Joseph C. Wong, Wayland Wong, David K. Woo, and Peter Yuen. *Completing the Face of the Chinese Church in America: The ABC Handbook Promoting Effective Ministries to American-Born Chinese*. Oakland, CA: Fellowship of American Chinese Evangelicals (FACE), 2009.

Engle, Richard W. "Contextualization in Missions: A Biblical and Theological Appraisal." *Grace Theological Journal* 4, no. 1 (1983): 85–107.

Fee, Gordon. *The First Epistle to the Corinthians*. The New International Commentary on the New Testament. Grand Rapids: William B. Eerdmans, 1988. In *Logos Library System* [CD-ROM].

Flemming, Dean E. *Contextualization in the New Testament: Patterns for Theology and Mission*. Downers Grove: InterVarsity Press, 2005.

Fong, Bruce W. *Racial Equality in the Church: A Critique of the Homogeneous Unit Principle in Light of a Practical Theology Perspective*. Lanham, MD: University Press of America, 1996.

Fong, Ken Uyeda. *Pursuing the Pearl: A Comprehensive Resource for Multi-Asian Ministry*. Updated ed. Valley Forge, PA: Judson Press, 1999.

Freeman, James M. *Manners & Customs of the Bible*. North Brunswick, NJ: Bridge-Logos, 1998. In *Logos Library System* [CD-ROM].

George, Timothy. *Galatians*. Vol. 30. The New American Commentary. Nashville: Broadman & Holman, 1994. In *Logos Library System* [CD-ROM].

Giles, G. N. "Church." In *Dictionary of the Later New Testament and Its Developments*, ed. Ralph P. Martin and Peter H. Davids. Downers Grove: InterVarsity, 1997. In *Logos Library System* [CD-ROM].

González, Justo L. *Santa Biblia: The Bible through Hispanic Eyes*. Nashville: Abingdon, 1996.

Grenz, Stanley, David Guretzki, and Cherith Fee Nordling. *Pocket Dictionary of Theological Terms*. Downers Grove: InterVarsity, 1999. In *Logos Library System* [CD-ROM].

Grudem, Wayne A. "Preface." In *Are Miraculous Gifts for Today?: Four Views*, Kindle ed. Wayne A. Grudem, ed. Counterpoints. Grand Rapids: Zondervan, 2011.

________. *Systematic Theology: An Introduction to Biblical Doctrine*. Leicester, England; Grand Rapids: Inter-Varsity Press; Zondervan, 2004. In *Logos Library System* [CD-ROM].

Harms, Richard B. *Paradigms from Luke-Acts for Multicultural Communities*. American University Studies. Series VII, Theology and Religion, vol. 216. New York: Peter Lang, 2001.

Hertig, Young Lee. "Reflections on the Inaugural Asian American Equipping Symposium." *SANACS Journal 2010: Society of Asian North American Christian Studies*, no. 2 (Sum 2010): 7–12.

Hesselgrave, David J., and Edward Rommen. *Contextualization: Meanings, Methods, and Models*. Pasadena: William Carey Library, 2000.

House, Paul R. "Suffering and the Purpose of Acts." *Journal of the Evangelical Theological Society* 33, no. 3 (Sept 1990): 317–30.

Janjaic, Vladimir, Christopher Brown, and Kevin Hammond. "Lapedo: Hybrid Skeletons for Programming Heterogeneous Multicore Machines in Erlang." In *Parallel Computing: On the Road to Exascale*, ed. Gerhard R. Joubert, Hugh Leather, Mark Parsons, Frans Peters and Mark Sawyer, 185-96. Washington, D.C.: IOS, 2016.

Jeremias, Joachim. *Jerusalem in the Time of Jesus: An Investigation into Economic and Social Conditions During the New Testament Period.* Translated by F. H. Cave and C. H. Cave. Philadelphia: Fortress Press, 1969.

Jeung, Russell. *Faithful Generations: Race and New Asian American Churches*. Kindle ed. New Brunswick, NJ: Rutgers University Press, 2005.

Jobes, Karen H. *1 Peter*. Baker Exegetical Commentary on the New Testament. Grand Rapids: Baker Academic, 2005. In *Logos Library System* [CD-ROM].

Johnson, Alan F. *1 Corinthians*. Vol. 7. The IVP New Testament Commentary Series. Downers Grove, IL: InterVarsity, 2004. In *Logos Library System* [CD-ROM].

Kang, S. Steve, and Megan A. Hackman. "Toward a Broader Role in Mission: How Korean Americans' Struggle for Identity Can Lead to a Renewed Vision for Mission." *International Bulletin for Missionary Research* April 36, no. 2 (2012): 72–76.

Keener, Craig S. *Acts: An Exegetical Commentary*. Vol. 2. Kindle ed. Grand Rapids: Baker Academic, 2013.

________. *Acts: An Exegetical Commentary*. Vol. 3. Kindle ed. Grand Rapids: Baker Academic, 2014.

________. *The IVP Bible Background Commentary: New Testament*. Downers Grove: InterVarsity Press, 1993. In Logos Library System [CD-ROM].

Khosrow-Pour, Mehdi, ed. *Dictionary of Information Science and Technology*, vol. 1. 2nd ed. Hershey, PA: Information Science Reference, 2013.

Kinnaman, David, and Aly Hawkins. *You Lost Me: Why Young Christians Are Leaving Church...And Rethinking Faith*. Grand Rapids: Baker, 2011.

Kluger, Jeffrey, and James Lovell. *Apollo 13*. Reprint ed. New York: Mariner Books, 2006.

Kraft, Charles H. *Christianity in Culture: A Study in Dynamic Biblical Theologizing in Cross-Cultural Perspective*. Maryknoll, NY: Orbis, 1979.

Land, Darin Hawkins. *The Diffusion of Ecclesiastical Authority: Sociological Dimensions of Leadership in the Book of Acts*. Princeton Theological Monograph Series, vol. 90. Kindle ed. Eugene, OR: Pickwick, 2008.

Laniak, Timothy S. *Shepherds after My Own Heart: Pastoral Traditions and Leadership in the Bible*. New Studies in Biblical Theology, vol. 20, Edited by D. A. Carson. Downers Grove: InterVarsity, 2006.

Lange, John Peter, ed. *A Commentary on the Holy Scriptures*. Bellingham, WA: Logos Bible Software, 2008. In *Logos Library System* [CD-ROM].

Law, Gail. "A Model for the American Ethnic Chinese Churches." In *A Winning Combination: ABC/OBC: Understanding the Cultural Tensions in Chinese Churches*, ed. Cecilia Yau, 131–41. Petaluma, CA: Chinese Christian Mission, 1986.

Lee, Franklin. "How to Encourage and Train More Local-Born Chinese

Ministers." In *Ethnic Chinese Congress on World Evangelization*, ed. Sharon Wai-Man Chan, 162–64. Tsim Sha Tsui, Hong Kong: Chinese Coordination Centre of World Evangelism, 1986.

Lee, Helen. "Silent Exodus: Can the East Asian Church in America Reverse the Flight of Its Next Generation?" *Christianity Today* 40, no. 9 (1996): 50–53.

Lee, Shelley Sang-Hee. *A New History of Asian America*. New York: Routledge, 2014.

Lenski, R. C. H. *The Interpretation of the Acts of the Apostles*. Minneapolis: Augsburg, 1961. In *Logos Library System* [CD-ROM].

Levine, Lee I. *Jerusalem: Portrait of the City in the Second Temple Period (538 B.C.E.–70 C.E.)*. Philadelphia: Jewish Publication Society, 2002.

Ling, Samuel, and Clarence Cheuk. *The "Chinese" Way of Doing Things: Perspectives on American-Born Chinese and the Chinese Church in North America*. Phillipsburg, NJ: P & R Publishing, 1999.

Lo, Eddie. "Body Life and Its Alternatives." In *Ethnic Chinese Congress on World Evangelization*, ed. Sharon Wai-Man Chan, 179–82. Tsim Sha Tsui, Hong Kong: Chinese Coordination Centre of World Evangelism, 1986.

Longenecker, Ricahrd N. *The Acts of the Apostles*. In Vol. 9 of *Expositor's Bible Commentary*, Edited by Frank E. Gaebelein and J. D. Douglas. Grand Rapids: Zondervan, Regency Reference Library, 1981. In *QuickVerse* [CD-ROM], (Grand Rapids, MI: The Zondervan Corporation, 1976.

________. *Galatians*. Vol. 41. Word Biblical Commentary. Dallas: Word, 1998. In *Logos Library System* [CD-ROM].

Love, Rick. *Muslims, Magic and the Kingdom of God: Church Planting among Folk Muslims*. Pasadena, CA: William Carey Library, 2000.

Lowe, Curtis to Ronald M. Rothenberg. "Discussion of Parallel Ministry." 25 October 2014, FaceTime.

Lukyanenko, D. V., and A. G. Yagola. "Using Parallel Computing for Solving Multidimensional Ill-Posed Problems." In *Computational Methods for Applied Inverse Problems*, ed. Yanfei Wang, Anatoly G. Yagola and Yang. Changchun, 49–64. Vol. 56 of Inverse and Ill-Posed Problems Series. Boston: Higher Education, 2012.

MacArthur, John F., Jr. *Ashamed of the Gospel: When the Church Becomes Like the World*. 3rd ed. Wheaton, IL: Crossway, 2010.

Marshall, I. Howard. *The Acts of the Apostles: An Introduction and Commentary*. Tyndale New Testament Commentaries, vol. 5. Reprint ed. Grand Rapids: William B. Eerdmans, 1989.

Martin, R. P. "Worship and Liturgy." In *Dictionary of the Later New Testament and Its Developments*, ed. Ralph P. Martin and Peter H. Davids. Downers Grove: InterVarsity, 1997. In *Logos Library System* [CD-ROM].

Mathison, Keith A. *The Shape of Sola Scriptura*. Moscow, ID: Canon, 2001.

Mauk, D., and J. Oakland. *American Civilization: An Introduction*. Reprint ed. New York: Routledge, 2005.

McGavran, Donald A. *Understanding Church Growth*, Edited by C. Peter Wagner. Grand Rapids: William B. Eerdmans, 1990.

McQuilkin, J. Robertson. *Measuring the Church Growth Movement*. Revised ed. Chicago: Moody Press, 1974.

Meeker, Barbara F. "Sociology." In *The Concise Encyclopedia of Sociology*, ed. George Ritzer and J. Michael Ryan, 599–602. Malden, MA: Wiley-Blackwell, 2011.

Metzger, Bruce Manning. *A Textual Commentary on the Greek New Testament*. 2nd ed. New York: United Bible Societies, 1994. In *Logos Library System* [CD-ROM].

Min, Pyong Gap. *Preserving Ethnicity through Religion in America: Korean Protestants and Indian Hindus across Generations*. Kindle ed. New York: New York University Press, 2010.

Minear, Paul S. *Images of the Church in the New Testament*. The New Testament Library. Kindle ed. Philadelphia: Westminster, 2004.

Mini-Consultation on Reaching Muslims (1980: Ban Phatthaya, Thailand). *The Thailand Report on Muslims: Report of the Consultation on World Evangelization Mini-Consultation on Reaching Muslims: Held in Pattaya, Thailand from 16-27 June 1980*. Lausanne Occasional Paper, vol. 13. Wheaton, IL: Lausanne Committee for World Evangelization, 1980.

Moltmann, Jürgen. *The Gospel of Liberation*. Translated by H. Wayne Pipkin. Waco: Word Books, 1973.

Montoya, Alex D. *Hispanic Ministry in North America*. Grand Rapids: Ministry Resources Library, 1987.

Mullins, Mark. "The Life Cycle of Ethnic Churches in Sociological Perspective." *Japanese Journal of Religious Studies* 14, no. 4 (1987): 321–34.

Neusner, Jacob, ed. *The Babylonian Talmud: A Translation and Commentary*. Peabody, MA: Hendrickson, 2011. In Logos Library System [CD-ROM].

________, ed. *The Mishnah: A New Translation*. New Haven, CT: Yale University Press, 1988. In *Logos Library System* [CD-ROM].

Ng, John L. "Church Models for Chinese Ministry." In *A Winning Combination: ABC/OBC: Understanding the Cultural Tensions in Chinese Churches*, ed. Cecilia Yau, 145-50. Petaluma, CA: Chinese Christian Mission, 1986.

Niebuhr, H. Richard. *The Social Sources of Denominationalism*. Hamden, CT: H. Holt and Company, 1929. Reprint, 1954.

Organization for Economic Co-operation and Development [OECD]. *A Profile of Immigrant Populations in the 21st Century: Data from*

OECD Countries. Danvers, MA: OECD Publishing, 2008.

Ortiz, Manuel. *The Hispanic Challenge: Opportunities Confronting the Church*. Downers Grove: InterVarsity, 1993.

________. *One New People: Models for Developing a Multiethnic Church*. Kindle ed. Downers Grove: InterVarsity, 1996.

________. "Foreword." In *A Future for the Latino Church: Models for Multilingual, Multigenerational Hispanic Congregations*, 43–60. IVP Academic, 2011.

Padilla, René C. "The Unity of the Church and the Homogeneous Unit Principle." In *Exploring Church Growth*, ed. Wilbert R. Shenk, 285–303. International Bulletin of Missionary Research Book Awards. Grand Rapids: W.B. Eerdmans, 1983.

Pai, Hyo Shick. "Korean Congregational Church of Los Angeles: The Bilingual Ministry and Its Impact on Church Growth." D.Ed.Min. diss., Fuller Theological Seminary, Pasadena, CA, 1987.

Parhami, Behrooz. *Introduction to Parallel Processing: Algorithms and Architectures*. Plenum Series in Computer Science. New York: Kluwer, 2002.

Parsons, Mikeal C. *Acts*. Paideia Commentaries on the New Testament. Grand Rapids: Baker Academic, 2008. In *Logos Library System* [CD-ROM].

Peters, George F. "Foreword." In *Contextualization: Meanings, Methods, and Models*, ix-xii. Pasadena: William Carey Library, 2000.

Peterson, David G. *The Acts of the Apostles*. The Pillar New Testament Commentary. Grand Rapids: W.B. Eerdmans, 2009. In *Logos Library System* [CD-ROM].

Phillips, Mercidieu. "Resolving the Causes of Second Generation Exodus from the Haitian Church in South Florida." D.Ed.Min. diss., Bethel

Seminary, Saint Paul, MN, 2011.

Philo of Alexandria. "Hypothetica: Apology for the Jews." In *The Works of Philo: Complete and Unabridged*, 742–47. Peabody, MA: Hendrickson, 1995. In *Logos Library System* [CD-ROM].

Polhill, John B. *Acts*. The New American Commentary, vol. 26. Nashville: Broadman & Holman, 1995. In *Logos Library System* [CD-ROM].

Proffitt, Michael, ed. *The Oxford English Dictionary Online*. Oxford: Oxford University, June 2016 [on-line]. Accessed 19 August 2016. Available from http://www.oed.com/view/Entry/7030? Redirected From=analogy&; Internet.

Ratha, Dilip, Sanket Mohapatra, and Ani Silwal. *Migration and Remittances Factbook 2011*. 2nd ed. Washngton D.C.: The World Bank, 2011.

Reisner, Rainer. "Synagogues in Jerusalem." In *The Book of Acts in Its Palestinian Setting*, ed. Richard Bauckham, 179–211. Vol. 4 of *The Book of Acts in Its First Century Setting*. Grand Rapids: William B. Eerdmans 1995.

Robinson, D. W. B. "Church." In *New Bible Dictionary*, ed. D. R. W. Wood and I. Howard Marshall, 199–202. Downers Grove: InterVarsity, 1996. In *Logos Library System* [CD-ROM].

Rodriguez, Daniel A. *A Future for the Latino Church: Models for Multilingual, Multigenerational Hispanic Congregations*. Kindle ed.: IVP Academic, 2011.

Schultz, Thom, and Joani Schultz. *Why Nobody Wants to Go to Church Anymore: And How 4 Acts of Love Will Make Your Church Irresistible*. Kindle ed. Loveland, CO: Group, 2013.

Schürer, Emil. "Alexandrians in Jerusalem." In *The Jewish Encyclopedia*, ed. Isidore Singer, 371–72. Vol. 1. New York: Funk & Wagnalls, 1906.

Shields, Brandon. "Family-Based Ministry: Shared Contexts, Shared Focus." In *Perspectives on Family Ministry: Three Views*, ed.

Timothy Paul Jones, 98–120. Nashville, TN: B&H, 2009.

Starling, A., ed. *Seeds of Promise: World Consultation on Frontier Missions, Edinburgh '80.* International Bulletin of Missionary Research Book Awards; 1981. Pasadena: W. Carey Library, 1981.

Stepick, Alex, and Carol Dutton Stepick. "Becoming American, Constructing Ethnicity: Immigrant Youth and Civic Engagement." *Applied Developmental Science* 6, no. 4 (2002): 246–57.

Strong, David K. "The Jerusalem Council: Some Implications for Contextualization Acts 15:1-35." In *Mission in Acts: Ancient Narratives in Contemporary Context*, ed. Robert L. Gallagher and Paul Hertig, 196–208. American Society of Missiology. Maryknoll, NY: Orbis Books, 2004.

Sullivan, Kathleen. "Catherine's Catholic Church: One Church, Parallel Congregations." In *Religion and the New Immigrants: Continuities and Adaptations*, Kindle ed. Helen Rose Ebaugh and Janet Saltzman Chafetz, eds. pp. 255–90. Walnut Creek, CA: Altamira Press, 2000.

Taylor, Matthew, and Jill Oliphant. *OCR Philosophy of Religion for AS and A2*, Edited by Jon Mayled. 3rd ed. New York: Routledge, 2015.

Thiselton, Anthony C. *The First Epistle to the Corinthians: A Commentary on the Greek Text*. New International Greek Testament Commentary. Grand Rapids: W.B. Eerdmans, 2000. In *Logos Library System* [CD-ROM].

Tousley, Nikki Coffey, and Brad J. Kallenberg. "Virtue Ethics." In *Dictionary of Scripture and Ethics*, Kindle ed., Joel B. Green, ed., K.l. 32472–663. Grand Rapids: Baker Academic, 2011.

Toussaint, Stanley D. "Acts." In *The Bible Knowledge Commentary*, ed. John F. Walvoord and Roy B. Zuck. Wheaton, IL: Victor Books, 1985. In *Logos Library System* [CD-ROM].

Tow, Peter. "How to Solve the Linguistic Problem in the North American

Chinese Church." In *Ethnic Chinese Congress on World Evangelization*, ed. Sharon Wai-Man Chan, 115–17. Tsim Sha Tsui, Hong Kong: Chinese Coordination Centre of World Evangelism, 1986.

Tran, Jonathan. "Why Asian American Christianity Has No Future: The over against, Leaving Behind, and Separation from of Asian American Christian Identity." *SANACS Journal 2010: Society of Asian North American Christian Studies*, no. 2 (Sum 2010): 13–36.

________. "Why Asian American Christianity is the Future: Holding It Together in Yellow Christianity." *SANACS Journal 2010: Society of Asian North American Christian Studies*, no. 2 (Sum 2010): 37–56.

Van Rheenen, Gailyn. "Reformist View: Church Growth Assumes Theology but Ineffectively Employs It to Analyze Culture, Determine Strategy, and Perceive History." In *Evaluating the Church Growth Movement*, ed. Paul E. Engle and Gary L. McIntosh. Zondervan Counterpoints Collection. Grand Rapids: Zondervan, 2004. In *Logos Library System* [CD-ROM].

Venkateswarlu, N. B. *Essential Computer and IT Fundamentals for Engineering and Science Students*. Ram Nagar, New Delhi: S. Chand, 2012.

Wallace, R. S. "Lord's Supper (Eucharist)." In *The International Standard Bible Encyclopedia*, ed. Geoffrey W. Bromiley, 164–70. Vol. 3. Grand Rapids: Wm. B. Eerdmans, 1988. In *Logos Library System* [CD-ROM].

Warner, R. Stephen. "Introduction: Immigration and Religious Communities in the United States." In *Gatherings in Diaspora: Religious Communities and the New Immigration*, Kindle ed. R. Stephen Warner and Judith G. Wittner eds., K.l. 18–459. Philadelphia: Temple University Press, 1998.

Weaver, Jason G. "Paul's Call to Imitation: The Rhetorical Function of the Theme of Imitation in Its Epistolary Context." Ph.D. diss., The Catholic University of America, Washington, D.C., 2013.

Webber, Robert. *The Younger Evangelicals: Facing the Challenges of the*

New World. Grand Rapids: Baker Books, 2002.

Weems, Lovett H., Jr. *Church Leadership: Vision, Team, Culture, and Integrity* Revised ed. Nashville: Abingdon, 2010.

Westminster Assembly. *The Westminster Confession of Faith*. Oak Harbor, WA: Logos Research Systems, 1996. In *Logos Library System* [CD-ROM].

Weston, Anthony. *A Rulebook for Arguments*. 2nd ed. Indianapolis: Hackett Publishing Company, 1992.

Wiarda, Timothy. "The Jerusalem Council and the Theological Task." *Journal of the Evangelical Theological Society* 46, no. 2 (2003): 233–48.

Witherington, Ben, III. *The Acts of the Apostles: A Socio-Rhetorical Commentary*. Grand Rapids: W. B. Eerdmans, 1998. In Logos Library System [CD-ROM].

Wolf, J. P. "Genre and the Video Game." In *The Medium of the Video Game*, ed. J. P. Wolf, 113–34. Austin, TX: University of Texas, 2001.

Wong, Joseph. "Dealing with Tensions in a Bi-Cultural Church." In *Ethnic Chinese Congress on World Evangelization*, ed. Sharon Wai-Man Chan, 148–49. Tsim Sha Tsui, Hong Kong: Chinese Coordination Centre of World Evangelism, 1986.

Wong, Joseph C. "The Biblical Basis for Promoting Effective ABC Ministries." In *Completing the Face of the Chinese Church in America: The ABC Handbook Promoting Effective Ministries to American-Born Chinese*, 17–23. Oakland, CA: Fellowship of American Chinese Evangelicals (FACE), 2009.

________. "Culturally-Sensitive OBC Leadership." In *Completing the Face of the Chinese Church in America: The ABC Handbook Promoting Effective Ministries to American-Born Chinese*, 75–100.

Oakland, CA: Fellowship of American Chinese Evangelicals (FACE), 2009.

________. "Is There a Future Need for ABC Ministries?" In *Completing the Face of the Chinese Church in America: The ABC Handbook Promoting Effective Ministries to American-Born Chinese*, 169–76. Oakland, CA: Fellowship of American Chinese Evangelicals (FACE), 2009.

Wong, Wayland. "Who Are the American-Born Chinese?" In *Completing the Face of the Chinese Church in America: The ABC Handbook Promoting Effective Ministries to American-Born Chinese*, 25-53. Oakland, CA: Fellowship of American Chinese Evangelicals (FACE), 2009.

Woo, David K. "Introduction." In *Completing the Face of the Chinese Church in America: The ABC Handbook Promoting Effective Ministries to American-Born Chinese*, 5–15. Oakland, CA: Fellowship of American Chinese Evangelicals (FACE), 2009.

________. "Planting ABC Churches." In *Completing the Face of the Chinese Church in America: The ABC Handbook Promoting Effective Ministries to American-Born Chinese*, 161–67. Oakland, CA: Fellowship of American Chinese Evangelicals (FACE), 2009.

________. "Power for Future ABC Ministries." In *Completing the Face of the Chinese Church in America: The ABC Handbook Promoting Effective Ministries to American-Born Chinese*, 177–88. Oakland, CA: Fellowship of American Chinese Evangelicals (FACE), 2009.

Yancey, George A. *One Body, One Spirit: Principles of Successful Multiracial Churches*. Kindle ed. Downers Grove: InterVarsity, 2003.

Yuen, Peter. "Parallel Ministries." In *Ethnic Chinese Congress on World Evangelization*, ed. Sharon Wai-Man Chan, 145–47. Tsim Sha Tsui, Hong Kong: Chinese Coordination Centre of World Evangelism, 1986.

________. "Effectively Promoting Missions among ABC Christians." In *Completing the Face of the Chinese Church in America: The ABC*

Handbook Promoting Effective Ministries to American-Born Chinese, 151–60. Oakland, CA: Fellowship of American Chinese Evangelicals (FACE), 2009.

Zaki, Zaki Labib. "'How Shall We Sing the Lord's Song in a New Land?': A Survey of the Needs and Challenges Facing the Educational Ministry of the Middle Eastern American Church." D.Ed.Min. diss., Chicago Theological Seminary, Chicago, IL, 1998.